THE
RETURN

A Biblical Study of End-Times

DALE AND CATHY HANCOCK

WESTBOW
PRESS®
A DIVISION OF THOMAS NELSON
& ZONDERVAN

WestBow Press books may be ordered through booksellers or by contacting:

WestBow Press
A Division of Thomas Nelson & Zondervan
1663 Liberty Drive
Bloomington, IN 47403
www.westbowpress.com
844-714-3454

Because of the dynamic nature of the Internet, any web addresses or links contained in this book may have changed since publication and may no longer be valid. The views expressed in this work are solely those of the author and do not necessarily reflect the views of the publisher, and the publisher hereby disclaims any responsibility for them.

Any people depicted in stock imagery provided by Getty Images are models, and such images are being used for illustrative purposes only.
Certain stock imagery © Getty Images.

Unless otherwise indicated, all Scripture quotations are from the ESV® Bible (The Holy Bible, English Standard Version®), copyright © 2001 by Crossway, a publishing ministry of Good News Publishers. Used by permission. All rights reserved.

Scripture quotations marked (NIV) are taken from the Holy Bible, New International Version®, NIV®. Copyright © 1973, 1978, 1984, 2011 by Biblica, Inc.™ Used by permission of Zondervan. All rights reserved worldwide. www.zondervan.comThe "NIV" and "New International Version" are trademarks registered in the United States Patent and Trademark Office by Biblica, Inc.™

ISBN: 978-1-6642-0391-4 (sc)
ISBN: 978-1-6642-0392-1 (e)

Library of Congress Control Number: 2020916778

Print information available on the last page.

WestBow Press rev. date: 10/20/2020

Dedicated to our three sons:

Adam, Joshua, and Jacob.

Your love for Jesus
and His Word inspires us

And to our daughters-in-law, Debbee, Mandie, and Emily. We couldn't love you more. The three of you embraced our family with all our passionate talk of God's Word and you all joined right in! What a blessing you are to our lives!

CONTENTS

PART 3: THE REVELATION

PREFACE

When you hear terms such as *the tribulation, Armageddon, the resurrection of the saints, the rapture, mark of the beast, martyrdom,* or *the Second Coming of Christ,* do you wonder what the sequence of events will be? Do you wonder how all these events fit together in God's plan for the ages? Do you wonder (and maybe worry) about what you and your loved ones will experience? Come along with us and let's take this journey together for His return is closer than ever before.

In this three-part study you will search the scriptures through the New Testament, the Old Testament, and finally, Revelation. There will be multiple-choice questions and fill-in-the-blank responses. There will be pictures to draw and charts to fill out. There will be sequence graphs and discussion opportunities. All you need is your Bible. The study is keyed exclusively to the English Standard Version (ESV) of the Bible.

However, we must give a word of warning. *Do not* start this journey unless *you* want to do the work. We aren't going to hand you the treasure; we are just going to show you the map. *You* will discover the treasure. Too often when studying end-times, we students simply recount the teachings of respected scholars and never research the Word for ourselves. This study is designed to show you where *you* can find the information in God's Word.

So be prepared. Using this travel guide will require some time and research on your part. But we hope it will be as exciting for you as it has been for us to discover the information in

on this treasure hunt to mine the depths and layers of Scripture for years. We would love to have you join us!

INTRODUCTION

Why should we study end times?

1. It is important to God.

There are hundreds of references in the Old and New Testaments of Christ's return. If it is important enough for Him to speak of something repeatedly, it is important enough for us to make the effort to understand it.

2. Jesus Himself urges us to watch, be on guard, and stay awake. Since we do not know when He will return, we could be found asleep and caught off guard (Mark 13:33–37).

We must not be lulled into complacency, but like the lesson of the fig tree, we must be aware of the season in which we live. Otherwise we will be like those in the days of Noah, who were eating and drinking, planting and marrying, and going on with their lives (Matthew 24:37-39). They lived without regard for the boat being built in the middle of the desert, without regard for the man Noah preaching truth and righteousness for years, and finally without regard for all those animals that curiously showed up two by two.

3. God *will* intervene in our lives one day; either this will be by death (which has happened to almost 100 percent of the population thus far), or we will be part of the privileged generation to live during the events that complete this age.

For that particular generation, the information found in God's Word will be of supreme and preeminent importance. It will be survival information for some.

Yes, this study will take some time. There are many verses to look up (it is exclusively keyed to the ESV version) and many trails to follow as a great deal of scripture is mined and cross-referenced. God is worth your effort, because ultimately this study is not about us.

It is about Him in all His glory, revealed as the King of kings and Lord of lords.

It is about seeing Him as He is, unveiled in majesty and judgment and amazing grace.

Three things to consider before we begin:

1. The embedded nature of the information

Wouldn't it be great if one book in the Bible contained all the end-times information, and we could simply read it in a concise, chronological order? When we began this journey, we thought Revelation was such a book. We were shocked. There was so much more we needed to understand, so many layers of information we still needed.

We came to realize that God, in His providence and with what we believe to be a divine sense of humor, placed the information throughout the whole of His Word, not just in one convenient location. Therefore, we must study the *entire* Bible to obtain a clear picture of the events of His return.

We have come to think of prophetic literature in terms of layers—layer upon layer of revealed truth, scripture commenting on scripture. It's much like the old anatomy books that layered colorful plastic pictures of bones, organs, muscles, vessels, and finally skin, one on top of the other, until the entire human body was revealed. Likewise, the study of prophecy involves layers of information, with many events throughout the scriptures occurring simultaneously. Finally, the last chapters of Revelation, the skin, wrap it all together.

2. Our high view of Scripture

We approach scripture conservatively, reading and studying it exactly as it says it is, the very Word of God: living, active, and sharper than a two-edged sword (truth).

The principle by which we interpret scripture, our hermeneutic, is plain and straightforward. It says what it says. Context, language, genre, figure of speech, and the commentary of scripture upon scripture are all taken into account in exegetical study.

We must be intentional and consistent with our interpretive principle. Otherwise we as students often accept God's Word at face value when it is easily understood and yet over allegorize the difficult, symbolic prophetic passages. The symbols in the apocalyptic portions represent real truth. A too-liberal handling of God's Word can diminish the truth and place us on a slippery slope, where the context in which we live is the interpretive barometer.

Recall that each and every prophecy of Christ's first coming was literally fulfilled, from His virgin birth to His crucifixion and resurrection. Logic follows that each of the prophecies of His Second Coming will also be literally fulfilled. So, rather than viewing the locusts, armies, and fires of Revelation symbolically, as things with which we are now familiar, such as helicopters and nuclear war, more likely those horrific locusts with human faces, those consuming fires, those deadly waters, and those one-hundred-pound hailstones are the result of God's wrath exactly as the Bible says.

The Bible is true and trustworthy. We must ask ourselves, *How honestly and seriously do I regard the Word of God? How seriously do I regard Him? Do I take Him at His word, or do I try to modify His Word into something more familiar or comfortable?*

The events of His return aren't going to be comfortable, but He is trustworthy and true, and He can be taken at His word.

3. Why does all this matter?

He is returning when God the Father says. There is nothing we can do about it, so why bother studying, especially since the subject is so ponderous and time consuming?

The truth is, studying this topic has the potential to completely change our perspectives on life. Seeing His sovereignty in the difficult days ahead is immensely comforting. He is the Alpha *and* the Omega, the beginning *and* the end. He is in total control; nothing will take place without His permission. There really is no fear in life *or* death. Living with the expectation that He really could return in our lifetimes will cause us to live more intentionally, more evangelically, and more victoriously.

Our study of the entirety of God's Word will become deeper and more personally engaging as we search His truths like the treasure they are, with riches there for us to find. The study will change our perspectives on our time, money, relationships, and the lost world.

Never will we appreciate our salvation so much as when we read of the wrath of God and from what (by His grace) we have been saved. Also, realizing the urgency of the days in which we live will hopefully spur each of us to share His good news more eagerly and fervently. The time is short, shorter than ever before.

Amen, come Lord Jesus!

CHAPTER 1

THE OLIVET DISCOURSE

We will now begin with the simplest, most clear exposition of Christ's return; the one in His own words, the Olivet Discourse. The disciples, like us, wanted to know what would be the sign of His coming and the close of the age as well as when the temple would be destroyed.

They were sitting with Him on the Mount of Olives, so His words to them became known as the Olivet Discourse. They may have been gazing across the Kidron Valley at the glorious Herodian Temple, having difficulty imagining its destruction.

He was about to be crucified, and these are some of His last words before He celebrated the Passover with them, instituting the Lord's Supper. He then *became* the Passover, the final sacrifice for our sins. This is critical information for His followers, and as such, it is repeated in each of the synoptic Gospels: Matthew, Mark, and Luke.

On the following page, you will find a chart comparing these passages. Beginning in Matthew 24, read verses 3–31 and place a mark in the corresponding box (we did the first ones for you) if you discover that term or event in the text. Then read Mark 13:4–27 and again mark the corresponding boxes in the chart. We will examine Luke 21 in the next chapter.

This is one of the more labor-intensive assignments in the whole workbook, but by completing this exercise, we will have carefully read the words of Jesus regarding His return. This discourse by Jesus is so important; we must begin by thoroughly understanding it.

Terms and Events

	Matthew 24:1–31	Mark 13:3–27	Luke 21:1–28
A. See that no one leads you astray; be on guard.	x	x	
B. Many saying, "I am the Christ/He," false christs, false prophets			
C. Wars, famines, earthquakes, pestilence, birth pangs			
D. Tribulation, persecution, hated for His name's sake, words given, witness empowered by the Holy Spirit			
E. Martyrdom			
F. Falling away, love grown cold, family betrayal unto death			
G. Gospel proclaimed throughout the world			
H. Abomination of desolation in the holy place/where he ought not to be			
I. Jerusalem, armies, trampled by Gentiles, desolation near			
J. Holy place (implied rebuilt temple)			
K. Survival information for those in Judea			
L. Concern for pregnant or nursing, pray not winter or Sabbath			
M. Great tribulation, cut short for the sake of the elect			
N. False christs/prophets—miracles and lies re: His return			
O. After great tribulation, sun, moon, stars affected/signs from heaven			
P. Return of Christ			
Q. All tribes of earth mourn, fear, foreboding			
R. Gathering the elect, rescue, redemption			

As you can see, Jesus's teaching in Matthew and Mark is very similar, sometimes word for word. Repetition in scripture is always an important sign to pay attention. Each time we read these passages, we are struck by the specificity, clarity, and chronology of the coming events as well as His sympathetic survival information for those in the hardest-hit place—Judea, Israel.

Were you struck by how bad conditions will be? It is chilling to read Jesus's words regarding betrayal within families, persecution, and even martyrdom. But just when it seems things couldn't get worse, He comes in the clouds and gathers His elect.

CHAPTER 2

JESUS'S TEACHINGS IN LUKE 21

In Luke 21, we find similar teachings by Jesus, but it isn't explicitly stated that He delivered them from the Mount of Olives, so we haven't designated them as such. Also, the only questions asked are when the temple will be destroyed and what the sign will be preceding that destruction. Because of this and other differences in the discourse, some scholars believe Jesus was addressing a different group, not His disciples. However, all three discourses include warnings, instructions, and encouragement for believers and conclude with His teaching on His glorious return in the clouds. This is an example of the layering of information as scripture is examined.

Read Luke 21:1–28. Return to your terms and events chart, and once again place a mark in the corresponding box if you find the statement. After you finish your chart, answer the questions below.

1. What is the main addition from Luke 21? Fill in the blanks.

   But when you see J_____ surrounded by a_____, then know that its d_____ has come n_____. (21:20)

2. What are the people in Judea to do?

   F_____[!] (21:21)

3. In Matthew and Mark, what is cited as the warning sign for those who are in Judea to flee? Fill in the blanks.

   So, when you see the a_____ of d_____ ... standing in the _____ place, (let the r_____ understand), then let those who are in J_____ f_____ to the mountains. (Matthew 24:15–16)

But when you see the a_____ of desolation s_____
where he ought n_____ to be (let the reader u_____), then let
those who are in J_____ flee to the m_____. (Mark 13:14)

4. In Luke, what event is cited as the warning sign for those in Judea to flee?

    When you see Jerusalem s_____ by armies. (Luke 21:20)

Whereas the books by Matthew and Mark speak of an event going on *in* the holy place, Luke's book refers to what is happening outside the city of Jerusalem with reference to the Gentiles. (Remember that Luke was a Gentile writing to Gentiles.)

Jesus gives layers of information regarding events that are occurring within the same time frame. He uses all the information to say at what point it is time to flee, to get out of town, and to run as fast as possible to a place of safety.

In Luke, we also see the reaction of the nations to the frightening signs in the sun, moon, and stars. People faint in fear and foreboding at the terrors and great signs from heaven. As the seas roar and the powers of the heavens are shaken, they will experience the end of the world as they know it.

5. But what are believers to be doing? Fill in the blanks.

    Straighten u____ and raise your h_____ because your
    r_____ is drawing n_____. (Luke 21:28)

What a powerful reassurance He gives to His own.

CHAPTER 3

EXAMINE YOUR KNOWLEDGE

Now that we have carefully read and rightly divided some of Christ's words regarding His return, let's examine our understanding of the discourse. Circle the correct response(s). (Hint: There is often more than one correct response; the answer key is at the end of the chapter.)

1. In Mark 13:5, why does Jesus say to see that no one leads you astray?

   a. Because false christs and false prophets will lead many astray.
   b. Because believers will be hated for His name's sake, and some will be put to death when they stand firm, and they could be tempted to cave in to deception.
   c. Because it will be a terribly difficult time, and He understands that believers will so long for His return that they could fall for the lies.

2. How do you think false christs and false prophets (plural) could prepare the lost world for *the* (singular) Antichrist?

   _____

   _____

   _____

3. In Matthew 24:8, why does Jesus compare war, famine, and earthquakes to early labor, the beginning of birth pangs?

   a. Because labor is warlike and feels like an earthquake.
   b. Because the beginning of labor may be indistinguishable from other contractions but closer to delivery (it is unmistakable).
   c. Because labor often begins slowly and gradually and then increases in intensity, becoming more and more powerful and profound before delivery.

d. Because an increase in the intensity of war, famine, and earthquakes, like an increase in the intensity of contractions, signals that the end is near.

4. Jesus speaks of some falling away in Matthew 24:10. What will that falling away entail?

    a. Betrayal by family members and friends.
    b. It refers to those who fall when the earthquakes occur.
    c. People who once seemed loving will no longer love but will be cold and hateful.
    d. People who once claimed to be Christians will deny Him.
    e. People will fall for the false christs and false prophets.

5. The Greek word for "testimony" or "witness" is *martyr*.[1] What did you notice actually precipitates the proclamation of the gospel throughout the world? (See Matthew 24:9, 13–14; Mark 13:9–11.)

    a. Television and social media
    b. The persecution and even martyrdom of believers
    c. The endurance of believers, their ability to stand firm in the face of betrayal, hatred, and lawlessness
    d. The Holy Spirit, who gives the very words to say when believers are brought before governors and kings

6. Can you think of other times in history when persecution increased the witness of the church?

    _____

    _____

7. What do we know about the abomination of desolation so far? (See Matthew 24:15; Mark 13:14.)

    a. It is standing in the holy place.
    b. It is standing where he ought not to be.
    c. It is spoken of in Daniel 9:27 and 11:31.
    d. It is a "he."
    e. When it is seen, those in Judea should flee.
    f. All the above

---

[1] Spiros Zodhiates, ed., *The Hebrew-Greek Key Study Bible*, New International Version (Chattanooga, TN: AMG Publishers 1996), 1648

8. Why does Jesus give such specific survival information to those in Jerusalem/Judea?
   (See Matthew 24:15–21; Mark 13:14–20; Luke 21:20–24.)

   a. Because the abomination of desolation is located there
   b. Because He is going to rain fire and brimstone down on it
   c. Because they are surrounded by armies
   d. Because the great tribulation now begins, and their lives are in danger
   e. Though the terrible conditions are worldwide, Jerusalem is the epicenter.

9. For whose sake is the tribulation of those days cut short? (See Matthew 24:22; Mark 13:20.)

   a. For the Jews
   b. For the elect
   c. For the lost
   d. For believers, both Jews and Gentiles

The word *elect* in the Greek is *eklectos*,[2] which means "picked out, chosen, selected." *Elect, elected, elect's,* and *election* occur twenty-three times in the New Testament; and with the exception of one reference to Christ (1 Peter 2:6) and one reference to elect angels (1 Timothy 5:21), all usages of *elect* refer to those who belong to Jesus, believers.

10. How is the tribulation of those days cut short? What events cut it short?
    (See Matthew 24:22-31; Mark 13:20, 24–27.)

    a. Jesus goes to the temple and kills the abomination of desolation.
    b. God suddenly turns off the natural light of the sun, moon, and stars.
    c. Jesus returns in the clouds in power and glory, and gathers or rescues His elect from the ends of earth to the ends of heaven.

11. What happens immediately *before* the Second Coming of Christ? (See Matthew 24:29.)

    a. A worldwide flood
    b. A worldwide hailstorm
    c. The sun and moon are darkened, the stars fall, and the powers of heaven are shaken.

12. What happens immediately *after* the tribulation of those days? (See Matthew 24:29.)

    a. A worldwide flood
    b. A worldwide hailstorm
    c. The sun and moon are darkened, the stars fall, and the powers of heaven are shaken.

---

[2] Zodhiates, *Hebrew-Greek Key*, 1618

13. According to Matthew 24:29–30 and Mark 13:24–26, Jesus has given us a sequence of the events surrounding His return. Circle the correct sequence.

   a. The Second Coming of Christ/the tribulations of those days/the sun, moon, and stars are affected
   b. The sun, moon, and stars are affected/the Second Coming of Christ/the tribulation of those days
   c. The tribulation of those days/the sun, moon and stars are affected/the Second Coming of Christ

Read the verses below regarding those who return *with* Christ.

Matthew 25:31: "When the Son of Man comes in His glory, and all the angels with Him, then He will sit on His glorious throne."

1 Thessalonians 3:13 "…so that he may establish your hearts blameless in holiness before our God and Father at the coming of our Lord Jesus with all his saints."

1 Thessalonians 4:13–14: "God will bring with him those who have fallen asleep."

14. Whom does Jesus bring with Him at His return?

   a. All his angels
   b. His saints
   c. Those who have fallen asleep, the dead in Christ
   d. All the above

The Greek word for "saints" is *hagios*,[3] meaning "holy ones." It is used to refer to angels and sometimes of believers. From all these verses, clearly He returns with His angels *and* those believers who already died.

15. Why do some people mourn and faint with fear and foreboding at His return. (See Luke 21:25–27.)

   a. The world has turned dark.
   b. The heavens are shaking.
   c. The seas are roaring.
   d. Then they see the Son of Man coming in a cloud in power and great glory.
   e. They are lost; they do not know Him.
   f. All the above

---

[3] Zodhiates, *Hebrew-Greek Key*, 1572

At this point in human history, there will be two groups of people: believers, who are gathered to Christ; and nonbelievers, who are left behind at His coming and to whom the world will seem to be falling apart. No wonder there will be perplexity, fainting, fear, and foreboding.

16. What are believers instructed to do when all the above events are taking place? (See Luke 21:28.)

   a. Hide in caves.
   b. Flee to the mountains.
   c. Straighten up and look up, "because your redemption is drawing near."

17. Imagine you are living when all these things begin to take place. How do you want to respond? How do you want your children and loved ones to respond? What can you do now to prepare yourself and them for the possibility and privilege of living during those days?

SUMMARY

So far, we know the Lord's return will be during very difficult times. Believers will be persecuted, betrayed by their families, and hated because of Him. Some will even be put to death. There will be an increase in false messiahs and prophets proclaiming false gospels with false signs, and even true believers will be tempted to follow. The world will seem to be falling apart with increasingly intense wars, famines, and violent earthquakes. Believers will have repeated opportunities to stand for Christ before religious and political leaders.

Then he, the abomination of desolation, will declare himself in the holy place, where he ought not to be, and Jerusalem will be surrounded by armies. At that point, conditions for believers (and for Jews who oppose him) will even worsen.

Jesus gives instructions that when the abomination of desolation (the Antichrist) is in the holy place, people should flee to the mountains. At just the right time, God will cut short or amputate the great tribulation of those days. He will darken the heavenly lights, and Jesus will appear in all His glory and majesty. He will gather His own to Himself, and His day, the day of the Lord, will begin.

Many godly and brilliant scholars think the discourses found in Matthew, Mark, and Luke were meant only for Jews because Jesus was speaking to His disciples, who were Jewish. This thinking would remove the church from experiencing the events Jesus described and asserts that they will be experienced only by new believers (probably mostly Jewish) after the church has been evacuated.

There is a problem with that view. It was those same Jewish men with whom Jesus would soon partake the Passover meal and institute the Lord's Supper, a church ordinance. It was those same Jewish men to whom Christ gave His Great Commission, the very battle cry of the church to go and tell the world the glorious good news of Jesus. And it was those same Jewish men who, fifty days after the resurrection, began the church on Pentecost.

On the Mount of Olives, Christ was speaking to His followers, all believers. He wanted His people to be prepared for the events surrounding His return.

It is also important to note that many of these events happened when the Romans destroyed Jerusalem and the temple in AD 70. What was a future event for His listeners at that time is now history for us. Like many prophetic portions of scripture, we see it already happened and will happen again. This is known as an "already-but-not-yet" event by some scholars.

However, the climactic event of that list, His return, has *not* yet taken place. Someday He will.

Answer Key:

1. a, b, c	8. a, c, d, e	13. c
3. b, c, d	9. b, d	14. d
4. b, c, d, e	10. b, c	15. f
5. b, c, d	11. c	16. c
7. f	12. c	

CHAPTER 4

THE LESSON OF THE FIG TREE

Immediately after Jesus explained how His glorious return would come about, He paused to teach a lesson based on the fig tree.

1. Read Matthew 24:32–35 (also Mark 13:28–31; Luke 21:29–33). Fill in the blanks.

   From the f_____ t_____ learn its lesson: as soon as its branch becomes t_____ and puts out its l_____, you know that summer is n_____.

His audience was familiar with fig trees. In fact, He may have been pointing to one while He was teaching. They could see the green leaves budding forth. After all, it was Passover, which happened every spring, the time for all the trees to begin to leaf out and bud.

Jesus explained that just as we can tell that summer is coming by observing the conditions prior to the season, there will be observable conditions prior to His coming. A budding tree serves as a sign of the season, an approximation of time that says summer is coming. It doesn't tell the day or the hour summer is to begin, but it promises the arrival of summer soon.

2. Read Matthew 24:33 (also found in Mark 13:29). Fill in the blanks.

   So also when you see all t_____ t_____ [taking place], you k_____ that h__ is n_____, at the very gates.

3. Read Luke 21:31. Fill in the blanks.

   So also when you s_____ these things taking place, y_____ know that the k_____ of G_____ is near.

4. Now, by allowing scripture to comment on scripture, and layering the information, to whom does the pronoun *he* refer? Who is *he*?

    J_____

He is Jesus because Luke uses the same context to say the kingdom of God is near.

5. What things are taking place? What is being seen that points to Him or His kingdom being near? Beginning with Matthew 24, make a list below of all the conditions that immediately precede these verses. Add additional information from each Gospel and check your list on the following page.

| Matthew 24:4–31 | Mark 13:5–27 | Luke 21:8–28 |

Here is our list:

Matthew 24:4–31	**Mark 13:5–27**	**Luke 21:8–28**
Wars and rumors of wars		
Famines		
Earthquakes		
Delivery to tribulation	Beaten in synagogues	
Many put to death	Empowered to witness by Holy Spirit	
Hated for His name		
Falling away of many		
False prophets led astray		
Lawlessness increased.		
Love of many grows cold		
Gospel proclaimed throughout world		
Abomination of desolation stands in holy place.	Jerusalem surrounded armies.	
Those in Judea flee.	Gentiles trample Jerusalem	
Increase in false messiahs and prophets		
Great tribulation like never before		
Great tribulation cut short for the elect sake		
The sun, moon, and stars affected		
Son of man comes in the clouds, earth mourns, elect gathered.	Redemption draws near.	

With the fig tree, certain conditions like tender branches and leaves signal that summer is near. With the return of Christ and His kingdom, when certain conditions are observable, they signal He is near. The list you just compiled reveals the conditions to signal that His coming is near. Very near.

In fact, Jesus goes on to emphatically assert a time frame regarding the nearness of His return when these things take place.

6. Read Matthew 24:34 (also found in Mark 13:30 and Luke 21:32). Fill in the blanks.

Truly I say to you, this g_____ will not p_____ a_____
until all t_____ t_____ take place.

The unique generation that experiences the terrible conditions of the last days will be the generation to whom the Lord returns. Think how comforting those words will be to that generation. This won't go on and on with no end in sight; He is coming back for the sake of the elect.

According to the words of Christ, true believers will experience tribulation and even great tribulation. The Greek word for "tribulation" is *thilipsis*.[4] It means pressure, crushed as with a weight—as in the olive press used to squeeze out the oil. It connotes burdensome anguish, trouble, and affliction. We are promised to be rescued from the wrath of God but not from tribulation or affliction.

In fact, in a non-eschatological context, in John 16:33 Jesus actually assured His followers that indeed we will have tribulation (*thilipsis*) in this world, but we should take heart; He has overcome the world.

Jesus gave us the wonderful encouragement that the manner in which believers experience the greatest tribulation in history will prove to be the greatest evangelical event in the history of the church, because the entire world will finally hear the gospel. The church will be given an audience as never before, as the world watches believers stand firm for Christ, even in the face of death. Faithful believers have been doing this over the centuries, but at this point, the persecution will be intensified and worldwide. Since we are given our very words by the Holy Spirit, the gospel will at last reach the farthest corners of the world. Then the Lord will return.

---

[4] Zodhiates, *Hebrew-Greek Key*, 1632

CHAPTER 5

NO ONE KNOWS THE DAY OR HOUR

No one knows the hour or day of Christ's return. In fact, Jesus said even He didn't know (Matthew 24:36). Anyone who asserts that he or she *does know* should be disregarded.

However, the no-one-knowing-the-hour-or-day mindset has led to the thinking that the return of Christ will be without sign, at any moment, and that it will catch everyone, even believers, off guard. Many of us were raised with songs like "What If It Were Today?" and "I Wish We'd All Been Ready," and many novels and movies have been based on a sign-less coming.

As we learned in the previous chapter on the fig tree, the Lord gave us an idea of the general season. He reassured us that the generation that those conditions met wouldn't pass away until they were all completed and He returned in glory. And as we will see, He warned us repeatedly not to be sleeping and caught off guard.

Read Matthew 24:36–44; Mark 13:32–36; and Luke 12:40. Circle the correct response(s) below.

1. Who does know the day and the hour?

    a. The angels
    b. The Son
    c. The Father

Only the Father knows the exact moment when He will send His Son to get His bride.

To exemplify no one knowing the exact hour or day of His coming, Jesus used the days of Noah as a comparison. Though Noah had been building that boat for over one hundred years and now animals were coming to him and getting *in* the boat, two by two, people went on with their lives.

2. We know from Genesis that the days of Noah were very evil, but what specific activities does Jesus mention the people were involved in when the flood came on them unawares (Matthew 24:37–39)?

   a. Eating, drinking, marrying, and giving in marriage
   b. Rape, murder, and sodomy
   c. Violence all the time

3. Are the activities of eating, drinking, marrying, and giving in marriage necessarily evil?

   a. Yes
   b. No

4. Why do you think Jesus compared the days of Noah to conditions at His return?

   a. They were eating and drinking to excess and engaging in polygamy.
   b. They were going on with their daily lives, doing things that involved a future.
   c. They weren't paying attention to Noah, his boat, his preaching, or the animals that walked calmly by them two by two.
   d. Their lack of awareness completely caught them off guard when the flood came.

5. Jesus also compared the situation at His return to that of a master who went on a journey and left his servants in charge (Mark 13:32–37). What is the main emphasis of what the master told his servants?

   a. Rest and go to sleep; it will be a long time before the master returns.
   b. Stay awake! The master could return at any hour.
   c. Continue to be about the work I assigned you.

6. Jesus has more to say regarding this attitude of readiness, comparing it to that of servants waiting for their master to come home from a wedding feast (Luke 12:35–40). Fill in the blanks.

   Stay d_____ for a_____. (12:35)
   Keep your lamps b_____. (12:35)
   And be "a_____." (12:37)

7. What will be the reaction of the master who finds his servants awake (Luke 12:37)? Fill in the blanks.

   He will dress himself for s_____ and have them r_____ at table and he will come and s_____ them.

Can you imagine? He will come and serve His servants.

8. Based on the above verses, what posture or attitude do you think we should have about His return? What is pleasing to Him? Circle correct responses.

   a. He is coming back at an hour I do not expect, so there is nothing I can do about it; why fret or concern myself with it?
   b. He is coming back at an hour I do not expect, but He has explained the conditions of that season, so I should be watching, noticing, eagerly expecting, and longing that He will come in my lifetime.
   c. I should quit my job and go wait for Him on a mountaintop.
   d. I should continue about the assignment He has given me in life, sharing His good news as I go.

9. How do you think the lost *and* the saved would live if they *did* know the hour and day of His return?

Lost people _____

Saved people _____

How would you live?

_____

_____

Jesus used two other familiar life events to showcase the confidence we can have in knowing an event will occur, even though we don't know the exact hour or day of that event, such as weddings and births.

from ours today. When a couple became engaged, the contract was legally binding; to break it, they actually had to get a divorce (recall Joseph's conundrum when he found out Mary was pregnant). However, they weren't to live together or consummate the marriage until the groom had their home ready.

He was to build that home adjoining his father's house. The bride waited day after day, probably always ready, maybe in a pretty dress with her hair done up nicely. She may not have known the exact moment he would come for her, but she could watch the signs as the house looked more and more complete. She knew he would come for her someday.[5]

---

[5] http://www.biblestudytools.com/commentaries/Revelation/related topics/Jewish wedding analogy.html

10. Read John 14:1–3. Fill in the blanks.

In my F_____ house are many r_____. If it were not so, would I have told you that I go to p_____ a place for you? And if I go and prepare a place for you, I will c_____ a_____ and t_____ you to m_____ that where I am you may be also.

Remember, the church is the bride of Christ. He is coming to get His bride and to take us to Himself.

Jesus also used labor and the eventual delivery of a baby when He compared the tribulation to the beginning of birth pangs (Matthew 24:8). Just as a pregnant woman doesn't know the day or exact hour she will give birth, she knows someday she will deliver her baby. As her time draws nearer, there are generally more and more signs in her body, more and more contractions or birth pangs. There may be false alarms before the day finally arrives, but one day after the intensity of the pangs becomes greater and greater, the baby will be delivered. One day after the intensity of the tribulation becomes greater and greater, Jesus *will* return.

Answer key: 1. c   5. b, c
2. a   8. b, d
3. b
4. b, c, d

CHAPTER 6

ONE TAKEN, THE OTHER LEFT

Read Luke 17:22–37. This is a different discourse regarding His return than the discourse of Matthew 24, Mark 13, and Luke 21. In this one, Jesus was *on His way* to Jerusalem with Pharisees around (Luke 17:11), whereas in the others, He was *in* Jerusalem, speaking with His disciples while looking at the temple.

1. How does this passage differ from the discourses you already studied in Matthew 24, Mark 13, and Luke 21? Circle the correct response(s) below (Luke 17:30–31).

    a. There is no survival information, no instruction to flee.
    b. There is no mention of the increasingly difficult conditions or the abomination of desolation and what they should do when those things are seen.
    c. There is no sympathetic concern for the pregnant and nursing women or that it should not happen in winter.
    d. Jesus told people to stay put, not to run.
    e. All the above

Why wasn't Jesus giving any survival information? Because at this point it will be too late. In this account, Jesus describes the day of His actual return, when the day of the Lord begins, not the day the abomination of desolation is revealed. Time will have run out. At this moment, one will be taken, and the other left.

Jesus compared that moment to the day Noah actually entered the ark and the day Lot escaped from Sodom.

2. What did God do for Noah and Lot (Luke 17:26–29)?

    a. He told them to hold on and pray.
    b. He kept them safe right where they were.

    c. He gave them manna and quail.

    d. He rescued them by removing them from the danger and destruction He was about to bring on the earth. He made a way of escape for them.

It is in *this* context that we read of the one-taken, other-left scenario. Just as Noah and Lot were taken out of harm's way, believers will be taken (gathered to Him) at His coming, and the rest of the world will be left behind to go through His day, the day of the Lord.

3. Read Luke 17:34–35. Fill in the blanks.

    In that n_____ there will be two in one b_____. One will be t_____ and the other l_____. There will be two women g_____ together. One will be t_____ and the other l_____.

4. Also read Matthew 24:40–41. Fill in the blanks.

    Then two men will be in the f_____, one will be t_____ and one l_____. Two women will be g_____ at the mill, one will be t_____ and one l_____.

5. What do these verses have in common?

    a. Jesus told of the activities both believers and nonbelievers would be involved with at His return.

    b. These activities assumed a future.

    c. The ones taken were taken away to some unknown place.

Because He used the comparison of the removal of Noah and Lot from danger, we can rest assured that those *taken* will be taken to safety.

6. How can it be night (two in one bed) for some and day for others?

    a. There will be a full eclipse of the sun.

    b. Some people work shift work.

    c. The return of Christ is a worldwide event, and the world is in half daylight and darkness all the time.

When Jesus returns, conditions on earth will be terrible, like those you listed from the Olivet Discourse. But the world will ignore the signs of the time and go on with their lives, engaging in activities that assume a future. Just as in the days of Noah, people continued eating and drinking and giving in marriage, while pairs of animals calmly walked into the ark with Noah and his family, and the flood caught the rest of the world unawares. Just as in the days of Lot, when not even ten righteous people could be found in Sodom, people continued to buy and sell, plant and build, until the moment when the angels dragged Lot and his family away and fire and sulfur rained down to destroy those left behind.

The one-taken, other-left scenario is used to emphasize the lack of watchfulness and awareness of prophesied conditions. It's not describing a secret, quiet, mysterious getaway or some kind of evacuation of evil out of the world. It portrays a profound urgency that one day He *will* return, and time will have run out.

Answer key: 1. e
                  2. d
                  5. a, b
                  6. c

CHAPTER 7

WHAT ABOUT THOSE LEFT BEHIND?

Those left behind at the coming of the Lord will go through His day, the day of the Lord, the wrath of God.

The purpose of the taking of believers isn't just to rescue them from the terrible tribulation they have been experiencing, the tribulation He cuts short or amputates by His return. The purpose is to rescue them from the wrath of God, which is about to commence on the whole world, the day of the Lord. With the exception of one hundred forty-four thousand chosen and sealed Jewish men (Revelation 7) and a remnant of Jews (the woman of Revelation 12), whom God protects in very unique ways (we will study this more in the Old Testament and Revelation portions of this workbook), the unsaved people, those left behind, will endure the terrible day of the Lord. We will see what specific events comprise the day of the Lord when we study the trumpets and bowls of Revelation.

But the apostle Paul had much to say regarding this most sober period in God's calendar of events.

Read 2 Thessalonians 1:6–10. Fill in the blanks.

1. What does He inflict on those who don't know God or obey the gospel of our Lord Jesus (2 Thessalonians 1:8)?

    "V_____"

2. When does He inflict vengeance on them (1:7)?

    When the Lord Jesus is r_____ from heaven with His mighty angels.

3. What will the lost suffer (1:9)?

   Punishment of e_____ d_____ away from the p_____ of the Lord.

4. Again, when will they suffer (1:9–10)?

   When He c_____ on that day.

5. When He comes on that day, what is He coming to do (1:10)?

   To be g_____ in His saints. And to be m_____ at among those who have b_____.

Recall that Luke 21:26 said people would faint with fear and foreboding and that Matthew 24:30 explained that people would mourn. Believers will joyously marvel at Him, and He will be glorified in them, but for those who don't believe, there will be judgment and vengeance.

6. Read 1 Thessalonians 1:10. Fill in the blanks.

   Jesus who d_____ us from the w_____ to come.

The day of the Lord will entail the wrath of God, something from which Jesus delivers His own. The Greek word for "deliver" is *rhuomai*,[6] and it means "to rescue, to preserve from." It conveys the idea of drawing someone out of a swift current or dragging a body on the ground away from danger. Jesus is going to rescue His church, removing her from earth immediately prior to the wrath that will begin at His return.

What a glorious day that will be for believers, but what a terrible day for those who aren't His. No wonder the study of His return should increase our evangelistic fervor. When the Lord returns, His day will begin—the day of the Lord, the wrath of God, the time of His vengeance, punishment, and judgment on planet Earth.

Peter also wrote of what would happen to those left behind at His coming.

7. Read 2 Peter 3:3–4. What will scoffers be saying?

   W_____ is the p_____ of His c_____?

8. Read 2 Peter 3:8–9. Why is God patient? He is allowing time for what?

   R_____

---

6 Zodhiates, *Hebrew-Greek Key*, 1670

But since the day of the Lord *will come,* believers should live lives of holiness and godliness.

9.   Read 2 Peter 3:10–12. What attitude should believers have toward the day of the Lord (v. 12)?

Believers should be "w_____ for and h_____ the coming of that day."

We as believers should be eagerly awaiting the coming day of the Lord.

Based on the above information, what conclusions can we draw regarding the state of affairs in the nonbelieving lost world versus the true church at the Second Coming of our Lord Jesus? Also recall everything Jesus already taught us in the Olivet Discourse.

_____

_____

_____

Prior to His coming, even though the world is experiencing great tribulation with wars, famines, plagues, and increasing deaths, the lost will go on in self-absorbed complacency, insisting that everything is going to be okay. "Peace and security," they will say, but time will eventually run out, and His inevitable coming and initiation of the day of the Lord will surprise them.

The true church will experience incredible persecution and even martyrdom, but they are to be at peace, knowing they aren't destined for God's wrath, encouraging one another, waiting with eager expectancy, longing for the day, and being diligent to be found without spot or blemish.

Then when He is revealed in the clouds, in power and in majesty, the world will mourn. Imagine the horror and fear and anguish amid the darkness and roaring, the earthquakes, and the heavenly bodies shaking and burning. And yet there will stand the believers, the true church, straightening up, looking up. They will be eagerly waiting, marveling, and glorifying our Lord Jesus as He comes—being rescued from the situation on earth but, more importantly, being rescued from the coming wrath of God.

CHAPTER 8

HE IS COMING LIKE A THIEF IN THE NIGHT

Many of us have been taught that Jesus will come secretively, unseen and unexpectedly, thief like, to snatch away the believers and then come gloriously in the clouds seven years later. Does the Bible actually teach that? His coming as a thief in the night has led many to that conclusion.

Therefore, we must examine all eschatological references to *thief*. The better question to ask is this: *To whom does He come as a thief?*

Jesus uses two thief analogies in the Gospels. They both involve the master of the house being ready or prepared for a thief.

Read Matthew 24:42–44 and Luke 12:39–40.

1. Based on these two passages, what seems to be the emphasis of Jesus's thief analogy? Circle all that apply.

   a. The world won't notice His coming back.
   b. For the unprepared and spiritually asleep, His coming will be unexpected. It will catch them off guard as a thief would catch the household asleep.
   c. His coming will be secretive and clandestine, thief like.

The whole world will very much notice His coming. It will be cataclysmic and anything but secretive. The lost world will be unprepared and caught off guard, and they may not understand what is happening (though some probably will), but it will be the end of the world as they have known it.

In fact, instead of a quiet, unseen event, Jesus likened His coming to a weather event that is very noticeable across the sky from the east to the west.

2. Read Matthew 24:27. To what does Jesus compare the visibility of His return?

L_____

Just as lightning is seen across the sky for miles on end, the coming of the Son of Man will be unmistakable; no one will miss it. The lost world won't be prepared for it and may misunderstand it, but His return will be noticed and will be catastrophic for planet earth.

3. As a matter of fact, Jesus tenderly warned His own against falling for a secret return. Read Matthew 24:24–26. Fill in the blanks. What will false christs and false prophets be doing?

Performing "great s_____ and wonders."

4. What will be the purpose of those signs and wonders?

To lead a_____ … the e_____.

Jesus assured us that He told us beforehand what would happen (Matthew 24:25), and then He went on to give a very specific warning.

5. Read Matthew 24:26. Fill in the blanks.

So if they say to you, "Look, he is in the w_____, do n_____ g__ o_____." If they say, "Look he is in the i_____ r_____, do not b_____ it."

Apparently, there will come a time when believers will so long for Christ to return that they will be vulnerable prey to the misleading lies of the enemy. Jesus knows this and has prepared us for it. He warned His followers not to be taken in by deception. His coming will be neither secretive nor quiet.

Now, in the book of Revelation (which we will study in part 3), there are two other situations in which Jesus states He will come as a thief.

6. Read Revelation 3:1–3. What does Jesus say to the church of Sardis?

I know your w_____. You have the reputation of being a_____, but you are d_____. Wake up … repent. If you will not w_____ u_____, I will come like a t_____, and you will not know at what h_____ I will come a_____ you.

These are chilling and sobering words by Jesus to an actual church. His coming *against* them at an hour they do not know, *as a thief*, is to a *dead* church in desperate need of repentance.

Read Revelation 16:15.

While describing the scene of the sixth bowl being poured out in preparation for the battle of Armageddon, Jesus gives a parenthetical warning. "Behold, I am coming like a thief! Blessed is the one who stays awake, keeping his garments on, that he may not go about naked and be seen exposed!"

7. What is His main admonition in both of these Revelation references?

   W_____ up!

We do not want His coming for us to be as a thief.

We want to be awake, aware, watchful, prepared, and about the assignment He has given us. We want to be a wide-awake church awaiting our Bridegroom.

It is actually Paul who uses the term "thief in the night."

8. Jesus's coming will be like a thief to nonbelievers, but what else comes as a thief (in the night)? Read 1 Thessalonians 5:1–2. Fill in the blanks.

   The d_____ of the L_____.

9. If Jesus speaks of His return as a thief and the day of the Lord coming as a thief, layering scripture upon scripture, what conclusion can you draw?

   _____.

The coming of Christ and the coming day of the Lord are one and the same. His return begins the period of time known as "the day of the Lord."

10. Read 1 Thessalonians 5:3. What are people (lost people) saying when the day of the Lord surprises them like a thief? Fill in the blanks.

    There is peace and s_____.

11. Do you think this peace and security are real? What happens to them while they are saying that?

    Then s_____ d_____ will come upon them as labor pains upon a pregnant woman, and they will not e_____.

Just as labor is the inevitable consequence of being pregnant, sudden destruction, with no way of escape, is the inevitable consequence of looking for peace and security in anything or anyone besides Jesus. The peace and security they proclaim (in the promises of the Antichrist) is false. The coming of Christ and His day surprises them like a thief in the night. But Paul went on to reassure the believers.

12. Read 1 Thessalonians 5:4–5. Does Jesus come for us (believers) as a thief in the night? Fill in the blanks and answer the question below.

But you are not in d_____, brothers, for that day to s_____ you like a t_____.

The answer is a resounding n____. That day should not surprise us like a thief in the night; we should be children of light, not of darkness.

The day of the Lord is a predetermined, divinely ordained period of time when the wrath of God will be poured out on this world. As 2 Peter 3:10 says, the day of the Lord *will* come.

13. Read 1 Thessalonians 5:9–11. Fill in the blanks.

For God has not d_____ us for w_____, but to obtain s_____ through our L_____ J_____ C_____, who died for us … therefore e_____ one another.

It is the wrath of God from which believers are spared, not tribulation. Thankfully limited by God, His wrath, as we will see when we study Revelation, will actually be much worse than the events you recorded from the Olivet Discourse. Those events comprise the tribulation and the great tribulation. When Jesus returns, He will rescue believers (who are still alive) and then initiate His day, the day of the Lord's wrath.

Answer key: 1. c

SUMMARY OF JESUS'S TEACHINGS ON THE FOLLOWING

- the lesson of the fig tree
- no one knowing the day or hour of His return
- His taking of one and leaving the other
- those left behind
- His coming like a thief in the night

Though no one knows the particular day or hour of Christ's return, just as the fig tree demonstrates signs that summer is near when it begins to bud and leaf out, the season of

Christ's return will be observable to those watching and noticing. Conditions will increasingly worsen and become life threatening when the abomination of desolation (the Antichrist in the holy place) presents himself. But because He told His believers what to watch for, the generation that sees these things will know their redemption, their rescue, is near, and they will be awaiting their Savior.

His return will be like a thief in the night for the lost, for those who are asleep, and for those who aren't awake and are unaware that prophetic events are being fulfilled right before their very eyes. The evacuation of believers, their being taken (their rescue), will seem abrupt, unexpected, and sudden to those left to go through the day of the Lord's wrath.

As we are seeing, not all the events of the last days are attributable to the wrath of God. As Jesus lovingly warned, His people will experience very tough days before the wrath of God begins. To be sure, He will rescue His church before His wrath, but there will be tribulation and terrible tribulation before His wrath begins. And as we will see in the Revelation portion, even the great tribulation pales in comparison to the wrath of God.

His coming as a thief in the night on a day and hour no one knows and His taking of one and leaving the other have given many the impression that He will come secretly and quietly. By examining those phrases in context and studying His own words, however, we see that His return for His own will be anything but clandestine.

To visualize the sequence of events thus far, it may be helpful for you to place what you have learned along a line. The middle * represents the midpoint of the seven-year period, the point at which the abomination of desolation is revealed (Daniel 9:27; Matthew 24:15). Place the terms and events on the line. (You can find a completed timeline at the end of part 1.)

CHAPTER 9

SIGNS IN THE SUN, MOON, AND STARS

As we studied in Matthew, Mark and Luke, Jesus told His followers that immediately *after* the great tribulation and immediately *before* His return, an amazing and frightening event would occur. The sun would be darkened, the moon wouldn't give its light, the stars would fall, and the heavens would shake.

To further demonstrate that the return of Christ will initiate the day of the Lord, this very conspicuous, one-time event is also said to precede the day of the Lord, as we will see in Acts 2 and Joel 2.

Ten days after Jesus's ascension into heaven, on the day of Pentecost, when the church began, Peter preached his first sermon. He opened with a quote from the Old Testament prophet Joel.

1. Read Acts 2:16–21 along with Joel 2:30–32. Fill in the blanks below (Acts 2:19–20).

    And I will show wonders in the heavens above and signs on the earth below, blood and fire and vapor of smoke; the sun shall be turned to d_____ and the m_____ to blood, b_____ the d_____ of the L_____ comes, the g_____ and magnificent day.

2. Read Joel 2:10–11. What does Joel add regarding the greatness and awesomeness of that day (2:11)?

    Who can e_____ it?

It is helpful to look at the descriptive terms *great* and *magnificent* in the Greek to get a fuller understanding.

Great in the Greek is *megas*,[7] from which we derive the term *mega*. It means "huge, mighty, and fearful."

---

[7] Zodhiates, *Hebrew-Greek Key*, 3489

Magnificent in the Greek is *epiphanies*,[8] and from it we derive the word *epiphany*. It means a memorable, conspicuous manifestation.

So, the day of the Lord is described here as a huge, mighty, fearful, memorable, and conspicuous manifestation of God. We will learn from the Old Testament that it will be a day of darkness and wrath.

Signaling us that the day is about to commence, God quite literally turns out the lights in the heavens. Then His Shekinah, His glory, is seen coming in the clouds, and He is here to begin His day.

3. Read Acts 2:16–21 and Joel 2:28–32. What is going on among God's people before the day of the Lord? (Remember, they will be under great persecution and tribulation.) Fill in the blanks.

    Who shall prophesy? "Your s_____ and d _____."
    Who shall see visions? "Your y_____ men."
    Who shall dream dreams? "Your o_____ men."
    On whom does God pour out His Spirit? "On a_____ flesh … even on male and female s_____."

To be sure, we have been in the last days since Christ's ascension into heaven and the Holy Spirit has inhabited all believers since the church began at Pentecost. But in the period of the *last*, last days, immediately before the day of the Lord, there will be ever-increasing manifestations and movements of God. He has always been drawing His people to Himself, but this will be a time of increased fervor, particularly, it seems, among the young—with sons and daughters giving proclamation of the truth and visions and dreams increasing. (God is increasingly using dreams and visions to call many to Himself, particularly in the Muslim world. We spoke with many missionaries in the Middle East, who recounted stories of people envisioning a man in white coming to them in love. They are then more receptive to hear of Jesus and trust Him as Savior.)

Lines will be drawn. Christianity will be less and less tolerated everywhere, yet the Bible tells us that Christians will become bolder and bolder, emboldened by the Spirit of God. True believers will have increased opportunity to witness before the politically and religiously powerful with the Holy Spirit giving them the very words to speak. The gospel will be proclaimed to the ends of the earth; all who are going to be saved will be.

Acts 2:21 tells us, "*Everyone* who calls upon the name of the Lord shall be saved" (emphasis added).

---

[8] Zodhiates, *Hebrew-Greek Key*, 2274

CHAPTER 10

THE ANTICHRIST

We have examined the revealing of Christ, known as His Second Coming. We have begun to examine the day of the Lord, the wrath of God, which will ensue at His coming. But before He comes, rescues believers, and initiates the wrath of God, another cataclysmic event will occur—the revealing of the man of lawlessness, the Antichrist.

How do we know he is revealed before Jesus returns? The same way the Thessalonians knew: by a letter from the apostle Paul.

Paul wrote the second letter to the Thessalonians to reassure them they were *not* living through God's wrath, the day of the Lord. The poor Thessalonians were enduring such affliction and suffering for their faith that they thought they had actually missed Christ's return and were experiencing God's wrath.

They had even allegedly received a letter from Paul that said as much (2 Thessalonians 2:2). Paul exhorted them not to be shaken or deceived and refreshed their memory of two conditions he had taught them when he was previously with them. He reassured them that those two conditions must be met before the coming of our Lord Jesus and the day of the Lord may ensue.

1. Read 2 Thessalonians 2:1–10. Fill in the blanks. What were the two conditions (2:3)?

   That day will not come unless the r_____ comes f_____,
   and the m_____ of l_____ is revealed.

The rebellion and the revealing of the man of lawlessness must occur *before* the "coming of our Lord Jesus and our being gathered together to Him" (2:1) and *before* "the day of the Lord has come" (2:2).

We will explore the rebellion later, but who is the man of lawlessness? Is he the Antichrist?

The common term *Antichrist* isn't actually used with the definite article in the New Testament. But Jesus referred to this character as the "abomination of desolation" (Mark 13:14). Paul referred to him as the "man of lawlessness" and "son of destruction" (2 Thessalonians 2:3), and Revelation calls him "the beast" (Revelation 13:5). In 1 and 2 John, John mentioned antichrist(s) several times as generally anyone who denies Jesus or His incarnation, and he mentioned the spirit of antichrist as being presently in the world in anyone who denied Christ. It seems that over the ages the church has coined the term "the Antichrist" to designate the ultimate embodiment of evil who is to come.

2. Read 2 Thessalonians 2:1–5. How does Paul describe this character (2:3–4)?

The son of d_____, who o_____ and e_____ himself against e_____ so-called god or object of worship, so that he takes his s_____ in the t_____ of God, proclaiming himself to be G_____.

3. Notice, where does he take his seat?

In the t_____.

4. And who does he proclaim himself to be?

G_____.

The man of lawlessness is indeed the Antichrist. He isn't just another false christ, of which there have been and will be many, just as Jesus taught us. This person is a unique character who will appear on the stage of human history at a specific time and place. He won't insist that he is the Messiah; he won't care about being Messiah. He isn't a *false* Christ or Messiah; he is the *anti*-Messiah. He will declare *himself* to be God as the man of lawlessness in the temple and will be the abomination that desolates it.

It is this event, his setting himself in the temple and claiming to be God, Jesus refers to in the Olivet Discourse as "the abomination of desolation standing where he ought not to be" (Mark 13:14). The Antichrist or man of lawlessness *is* the abomination in the temple, and his presence and proclamation there will desolate it.

This revealing of the man of lawlessness will take place at a specific point in time. Jesus told us in Matthew 24:15 that the prophet Daniel spoke of this character. Daniel told us when the abomination that desolates the temple will be revealed.

Read Daniel 9:27 below (a very difficult verse). We have recorded it from the New International Version (NIV) because the syntax is a bit easier to follow. Read it also in the King James Version

(KJV), New American Standard Bible (NASB), and Holman Christian Standard Bible (HCSB) as well as the ESV.

> He will confirm a covenant with many for one "seven" [seven years] In the middle of the "seven", he will put an end to sacrifice and offering. And on a wing of the temple, he will set up an abomination that causes desolation, until the end that is decreed is poured out on him.

This abominable character, the Antichrist, the man of lawlessness, will make a seven-year covenant, presumably with Israel. Somehow the sacrificial system will resume, something that up to this time had been impossible in light of the present Muslim occupation of the Temple Mount. We know it resumes because halfway through that seven-year agreement, he will break the covenant he made and force the people to stop their sacrifices and offerings in the (apparently rebuilt) temple. At that point he will set himself up in that temple and desolate it. Thus, from Daniel we know the Antichrist will be revealed for who he is three and a half years into the seven-year covenant.

Paul went on in his second letter to the Thessalonians to give more warning information on the man of lawlessness and the power behind him.

5. Read 2 Thessalonians 2:9–10. Who totally empowers the Antichrist?

   S_____.

6. What is he empowered to do?

   False s_____ and w_____.

7. Who will fall prey to his wicked deception?

   Those who are p_____ because they r_____ to l_____ the truth and so be s_____.

The Antichrist will be able to perform miraculous and amazing things, signs and wonders that will deceive the world. It is no wonder that Jesus repeatedly warned believers to see to it that they weren't led astray. True believers won't follow this satanically indwelt anti–Messiah, the counterfeit, even with all his signs and wonders. Believers won't be deceived because they love the truth, and so we must *know* the truth (Mark 13:21–23).

Satan's work in this world is nothing new, but this will be different. This is the devil's cheap copy of the incarnation—the Satan man. We will learn much more about this character in our study of the Old Testament prophets and Revelation.

CHAPTER 11

THE TEMPLE AND THE RESTRAINER

At the time of this writing, there is no temple in Jerusalem. The Romans destroyed the last temple, often called the "second temple" or the "Herodian Temple" in 70 AD. Presently, on what Jews and Christians still know as the Temple Mount, there are two Muslim worship sites, El Aqsa mosque and the Dome of the Rock, with its iconic gold-clad dome.

1. Read Mark 13:14 and fill in the blanks.

   But when you see the abomination of desolation s_____ where h____ ought n_____ to be (let the reader understand).

2. Read Matthew 24:15 and fill in the blanks.

   So when you see the abomination of desolation spoken of by the prophet Daniel, s_____ in the h_____ p_____ (let the reader understand).

3. Read 2 Thessalonians 2:3–4 and fill in the blanks.

   That day will not come unless the man of l_____ is revealed ... so that he takes his seat in the t_____ of God, proclaiming himself to be God.

Based on the above three verses, fill in the blanks to complete the following equation.

W_____ he ought n_____ t____ be = h place = t_____

The man of lawlessness, the abomination of desolation or the Antichrist, as we call him, will set himself in *the holy place, the temple, where he ought not to be.* For him to do so, a temple, the third temple, often called the "Tribulation Temple," must be rebuilt. As such, though implied and not explicit, it would seem that a temple on the Temple Mount in Jerusalem is another condition to be met before the return of Christ.

The Bible doesn't tell us how such a temple could be rebuilt. Amid the present-day tension between Jews and Muslims, it's quite difficult to imagine such a thing ever taking place. But there are presently many in Israel who are preparing for such an event. We recently visited the Temple Institute in the Old City of Jerusalem. They have recreated copies of the temple furnishings: the altar of sacrifice, the laver, the table of shewbread, the altar of incense, and the beautiful golden menorah, which stands under bulletproof glass in the center of the Jewish Quarter. They have made the vestments for the high priest with the jewel-embedded ephod and materials dyed from tiny worms and snails, just like the materials the Israelites plundered from the Egyptians to fashion Aaron's garments. They are ready. They even claim to know where the ark of the covenant is. Yet the ark was never present in the second temple, so it would seem that sacrifices could be reinstituted even without it. They have all the other furnishings that were present in the original tabernacle when God instituted the sacrificial system.

We believers know that the sacrificial system is no longer necessary—that Jesus was the final, perfect Lamb of God. Jesus completed and finished the sacrificial system. But it seems that these observant Jews in Jerusalem, who don't recognize Jesus, Yeshua, as their Messiah, will have an instrumental role to play in this portion of the prophetic events.

It may be a small temple, tabernacle sized; one can only speculate with a divinely enhanced imagination of how this will come about. As we watch the ever-increasing tension and fighting throughout the Middle East, the Temple Mount, known as the "Noble Sanctuary" to the Muslims, the most valuable thirty-six acres of real estate in the world, continues to be increasingly in the news.

But according to Daniel 9:27, Jewish sacrificial worship *will be* reinstated and then forbidden by the one who initiates a covenant and then forces the sacrifices to end, setting up an abominable desolation. This presupposes a temple, and it must be located where the first two were—on Mt. Moriah, where Abraham was willing to sacrifice Isaac and where David bought the threshing floor to stop the plague of 2 Samuel 24. Solomon's temple was there until the Babylonians destroyed it in 586 BC, and the second temple was built there when the captives returned. Herod enlarged it and the surrounding mount to the present thirty-six acres it is today. The Romans destroyed that temple in AD 70.

Let's examine another character God uses, the restrainer.

4. What pronoun is used of the restrainer? Read 2 Thessalonians 2:5–8 and fill in the blank.

   H____.

God will remove the restrainer, a divinely appointed *he*, someone who has been keeping these events at bay until the proper time—when God allows.

This is the only mention of the *restrainer* in the New Testament, and we will further explore this character in the Daniel portion of the study.

Restrain in the Greek is *katecho*,[9] which means "to hold back, hold down, hold fast, or prevent." It is an intense word for hinder or delay. One can almost picture the restrainer holding the Antichrist's arms behind his back through the centuries … until God has the restrainer stop restraining.

5. When will the lawless one be revealed? Read 2 Thessalonians 2:7 and fill in the blanks.

When the restrainer is taken "o_____ of the w_____.

God is totally in control. He will permit these events to begin, and He will end them at their proper time. As powerful and horrific as the Antichrist is going to be, he is a dead man walking. His end is already sure. God is holding him at bay with His restrainer. Someday the restrainer will be taken out of the way, and the unrestrained Antichrist will lunge onto the scene.

6. How does Jesus kill him (2:8)?

With the b_____ of His m_____ and bring to n_____.

The Antichrist is no match for our Savior and King.

SEQUENCE OF EVENTS

To help organize what we know so far, renumber the following events in their proper order.

1. Restrainer out of the way
2. Second Coming of Christ
3. Tribulation
4. Man of lawlessness revealed in the temple/abomination of desolation/where he ought not to be
5. Signs in the sun, moon, stars, and heavens
6. Day of the Lord
7. Great tribulation

The sequence is as follows: 3, 1, 4, 7, 5, 2, 6.

---

[9] Zodhiates, *Hebrew-Greek Key*, 1640

The tribulation turns into the great tribulation when the restrainer stops restraining and the man of lawlessness is revealed as the abomination that desolates the (rebuilt) temple. His evil presence there causes great tribulation for believers. When it becomes so bad that if it weren't cut short, no one would be left alive, God turns out the lights in the heavens, and Jesus returns in glory and begins His day, the day of the Lord.

Again, if it helps to visualize these events in a linear manner, place them on the sequence line below. We don't know when events like the return of Christ will occur, nor do we know the duration of the great tribulation or the day of the Lord; we know only the sequence.

CHAPTER 12

THE REBELLION OR APOSTASY

1. When Paul wrote a second time to the church at Thessalonica, how did he reassure them that they hadn't missed the coming of the Lord and their being gathered to Him? What did he remind them was the first prerequisite to the coming of the day of the Lord? Read 2 Thessalonians 2:3 and fill in the blank.

   The r_____.

The Greek word for *rebellion* is *apostasia*.[10] This word, used only twice in the New Testament, means "apostasy, to apostatize, to fall away from, to defect from, to turn away from the truth."

It is difficult to say whether this rebellion is a specific event or the general atmosphere of the day. Paul didn't elaborate on it, but he did use the definite article "the" to reference it—*the* rebellion. It's almost as though Paul assumed his audience knew exactly what he was talking about, but we don't.

2. From our study so far, can you think of any descriptions of behaviors that would qualify as this rebellion? Read Matthew 24:10–12 and fill in the blanks.

   h_____ one another.

   And because l_____ will be increased, the love of many will grow c_____.

The Greek word for the term "fall away" is *skandalizo*,[11] and it means "to cause to stumble and fall." Jesus seemed to be describing conditions of apostasy, of turning from the one true God, prior to His coming.

---

10 Zodhiates, *Hebrew-Greek Key*, 1591
11 Zodhiates, *Hebrew-Greek Key*, 1671

3. Read Mark 13:12–13 and fill in the blanks.

And brother will deliver b_____ over to death, and the father his c_____, and children will rise against p_____ and have them put to d_____. And you will be h_____ by all for my n_____ sake. But the one who endures to the end will be saved.

It is difficult to imagine such a time of betrayal and hatred with family members turning on one another and children having their parents put to death. It's very plausible that Jesus is describing the rebellion and apostasy of which Paul speaks.

We find more elaboration on this unique period of apostasy in the last days in Paul's letters to Timothy.

4. Read 1 Timothy 4:1 and fill in the blanks.

Now the Spirit expressly says that in later times some will d_____ from the faith by devoting themselves to deceitful s_____ and teachings of d_____.

The Greek word for "depart" is *aphistemi*; it implies that the allegiance to the truth that was once professed is now denied.[12]

5. Because terms like "fall away, turn away, and depart from" are used, based on all the above passages, from which group do you think the rebellion will originate?

a. People who once professed to be Christians; nice, respectable, trusted people; probably members of a church
b. People who never professed Christianity, the non-believing, lost world

It appears that the rebellion, betrayal, and falling away will be from within our own families and churches. It will be a heart-wrenching, agonizing time; and because of its apparent scope, it will be a unique time in the history of the church.

You may be asking yourself, "Could I fall away? Could I forsake the truth? Could I be apostate and turn from Him?"

The resounding answer is, "No! Not if you truly belong to Him." Salvation is by His grace through faith, a gift freely received; He is not going to take it back. We cannot lose our salvation, but we can certainly choose to live less than victoriously.

The coming days won't be easy. Believers will not only be persecuted and hated. They will first be betrayed, mocked, discredited, and marginalized by the world.

---

[12] Zodhiates, *Hebrew-Greek Key*, 1597

They will be betrayed by the lost world *and* by those who have proclaimed to be Christians but never truly were. The atmosphere that will pervade during the rebellion will be horrible for true believers. We and generations after us must be firmly rooted in the Word and deeply grounded in our faith to be ready to stand for Christ in the coming difficult days.

In his second letter to Timothy, Paul exhorted Timothy to understand the impending times of difficulty and the types of people who will creep in and corrupt in the last days.

6. Read 2 Timothy 3:1–9 and make a list of the characteristics found in verses 2–5. You will find our completed list below yours.

Characteristics of people in the last days:

Here is our list:

Characteristics of people in the last days:

1. Lovers of self
2. Lovers of money
3. Proud
4. Arrogant
5. Abusive
6. Disobedient to parents
7. Ungrateful
8. Unholy
9. Heartless
10. Unappeasable
11. Slanderous
12. Without self-control
13. Brutal
14. Not loving the good
15. Treacherous
16. Reckless
17. Swollen with conceit
18. Lovers of pleasure rather than God
19. Having appearance of godliness but denying its power

People have always had the traits we just listed; they are the result of our fallen nature. But Paul warned Timothy and us that in the last days there will be an escalation in the intensity of the evil to which mankind is capable.

This also serves as a good checklist for us as believers, by which we can examine ourselves, confess any of these ungodly traits, repent, and turn from them.

CHAPTER 13

THE RAPTURE

The word *rapture* isn't in the Bible. The event, however, is referred to with many terms—"gathering," "being caught up," and "delivering from." The rapture is a rescue for those believers who are still alive, a rescue from the terrible time of tribulation they are in and from the wrath of God, which is about to begin. At the Second Coming of Christ, He will first resurrect the dead believers, gather up the living ones, and pour out His wrath during the day of the Lord.

This gathering is the rapture. We know this by letting scripture comment on scripture.

Matthew 24:31 says that after the tribulation and the sun and moon are darkened, Jesus will come in the clouds to "*gather* his elect" (emphasis added). Mark 13:27 says He will send His angels to "*gather* His elect" (emphasis added). And Paul wrote, "Concerning the coming of our Lord Jesus and our being *gathered* together to Him" (2 Thessalonians 2:1, emphasis added).

The Greek word for "gather" is *episunago*.[13] It means "to collect, to have a complete collection, to assemble together." It is used only in three other places in the New Testament, one in which Jesus lamented over Jerusalem and tenderly longed to gather her as a hen gathers her brood (Matthew 23:37).

As we have read and recorded what will happen during the tribulation and the great tribulation, it is no wonder that believers will be longing to be gathered to Him as a complete collection, rescued.

1. You can probably fill in the blanks of Matthew 24:21–22 from memory.

   For then there will be g_____ t_____, such has n_____ b_____ from the beginning of the world until n_____, no and

---

[13] James Strong, *The New Strong's Exhaustive Concordance of the Bible* (Nashville: Thomas Nelson Publishers, 1995), 1996

n_____ w_____ be. And if those days had not been c_____
s_____, no human being would be saved. But for the sake of the
e_____ those days will be c_____ s_____.

The great tribulation will be a time in the history of the world like never before. If it is allowed to go on, no one will survive. But God is in control, and He will cut it short. The Greek word for "cut short" is *koloboo*,[14] which means "to cut off, amputate, or shorten."

It's important to note that the great tribulation begins at the midpoint of the last seven-year allotted portion of time for this age, but it doesn't last for the entire second half; it is "cut short" (Matthew 24:21–22).

2. For whose sake does God shorten the great tribulation?

   For the e_____.

How does He shorten it? How does He cut it off? By His return. And His first order of business is to gather His own.

3. Read Matthew 24:29–31 and fill in the blanks, again probably from memory.

   Immediately after the t_____ of those days … they will see the Son of Man c_____ on the c_____ of heaven … And He will send out His angels with a loud trumpet call, and they will g_____ His e_____ from the four winds, from one end of heaven to the other.

4. Why does He come and shorten the great tribulation? Read 1 Thessalonians 1:10 and fill in the blanks.

   And to wait for His Son from heaven, whom He raised from the dead, Jesus who d_____ us from the w_____ to come.

The Greek word for "deliver" is *rhuomai*, which means "to rescue, as though dragging a body from certain danger." The rapture of the church is a rescue—out of the great tribulation and from the wrath to come. The great tribulation is shortened by Christ's return and the rescue of God's elect because for the remainder of the allotted 7 years, the world will experience the wrath of God, the day of the Lord.

5. Read 1 Thessalonians 4:16–18. Let's look at the sequence of events of that glorious moment of rapture.

---

[14] Zodhiates, *Hebrew-Greek Key*, 2088

The Lord Himself will descend from heaven with what three sounds?

   a. A cry of c_____
   b. The voice of an a_____
   c. The sound of the t_____ of God

6. Then what four things occur and in what order? Number the events below in their proper sequence.

   a. "Meet the Lord in the air"
   b. "The dead in Christ rise first"
   c. "All be with the Lord"
   d. "Then we who are a_____, who are l_____, will be c_____ u_____ with them [the resurrected dead] in the c_____."

You should have b, d, a, c.

7. What should these words accomplish among believers?

   E_____t!

It's no wonder that Paul says to encourage one another with these words. This catching up in the air will be such a glorious homecoming. And just in time.

Rescued from the wrath of God and out of the terrible conditions of the great tribulation, living believers will be gathered to Him, meeting the saints who have gone before.

Something else wonderful occurs at this moment. We get a new body, something we long for more and more as we age.

8. Read 1 Corinthians 15:50–53 and fill in the blanks.

   We shall not all s_____ [die], but we shall all be c_____, in a moment, in the t_____ of an eye … the trumpet will sound and the dead will be r_____ imperishable, and we [the living] will be changed. For this perishable body must put on the i_____ and this mortal body must put on i_____.

"Flesh and blood cannot inherit the kingdom of God," so we must be changed into immortal, imperishable bodies. The dead are raised with their immortal bodies, and those still left alive are also changed instantly into immortal bodies. It's a lot to happen in the twinkling of an eye, but our God can do anything.

CHAPTER 14

THE RESURRECTION OF THE DEAD IN CHRIST

1. Read 1 Thessalonians 4:13–15 and fill in the blanks. What group were the Thessalonians uninformed about?

    Those who are a_____.

Because they were uninformed, what were they doing?

    Grieving as others do who h_____ no h_____.

The poor Thessalonians thought their loved ones who had died before the coming of the Lord had missed out on the resurrection. Paul wrote to explain how things really were and that though they grieved, they shouldn't do so as those who have no hope.

2. They now have a glorious hope because at the coming of the Lord, whom will He bring with Him (1 Thessalonians 4:14)?

    Those who have f_____ a_____.

    Who will not precede those who have fallen asleep?

    We who are a_____, who are l_____ until the coming of the Lord.

Many in the church at Thessalonica were Gentile believers and previous pagans. In their minds, death was to be viewed with horror, with hopelessness, as the cessation of existence. Paul wrote to reassure them that their loved ones who had died in Christ were with Him and were going to experience resurrection just as Jesus had risen again.

3. Read 1 Thessalonians 4:16–18 and fill in the blanks.
    When the Lord descends from heaven, who rises to meet Him first?

    The d_____ in C_____.

Who goes up next?

    We who are a_____, who are left.

(Interestingly, the word for *left* has the connotation of just hanging on, barely surviving, remaining.)

Now we have a bit of a conundrum. The dead in Christ come back with Him … and they rise first?

Yes and yes.

Recall that when we die, we are immediately in the presence of the Lord (2 Corinthians 5:6–8; Philippians 1:21–22), but we don't yet have our glorified bodies. Though our dead loved ones are in His presence, no one has his or her new, immortal body until Christ returns.

4. What is the purpose of our being given a glorified body? Why is this necessary? Read 1 Corinthians 15:50–58 and fill in the blanks.

    Because flesh and blood cannot i_____ the kingdom of God. (15:50)
    Because the perishable must p_____ o_____ the imperishable. (15:53)
    Because the mortal must p_____ o_____ immortality. (15:53)
    Like a beautiful new suit, we must put on an immortal, imperishable body for our ultimate inheritance.

5. How fast does all this happen?

    a. It will take years, maybe some time in purgatory.
    b. This transition will occur in heaven, while the wrath of God is being poured on the earth.
    c. It will take but the twinkling of an eye.

Like Paul said, it is a mystery, but it will happen. Imagine, at the height of extreme difficulty, amid even the martyrdom of some, when the world seems to be falling apart, our Redeemer, our Rescuer, our Savior will come.

His angels accompany Him as well as His saints (our dead loved ones and all the believers throughout the ages). They are somehow reunited with their bodies as they rise from the ground, changed into beautiful, perfect physical versions of themselves, immortal and imperishable. Then those who are still alive, seemingly hanging in there until His return, will be transformed also into immortal, imperishable ones and rise to meet Jesus and those who went before. Oh, what glory—to forever be with Him and all the believers throughout the ages in glorified, perfect, immortal bodies, in perfect fellowship with Him and one another, incapable of sin, and never again to be subject to sorrow, disease, pain, or death.

6. What will our new bodies be like? Read 1 John 3:1–3 and circle the correct response.

   a. The angels
   b. Like Moses and Elijah at the transfiguration
   c. Like Jesus

7. Read Philippians 3:20–21 and fill in the blanks.

   We await a Savior, the Lord Jesus Christ, who will t_____ our l_____ body to be like h_____ g_____ body.

Our bodies will actually be like Jesus's. Imagine. One day He will pull us into His very presence, and we will see Him as He is. He will change us into immortal image bearers, incapable of sin. Oh, the sweetness of the communion that is to come.

CHAPTER 15

THE JUDGMENT, JUDGMENT DAY

1. Read Hebrews 9:27–28 and fill in the blanks.

   And just as it is appointed for man to d_____ once, and after that comes j_____, so Christ, having been offered once to bear the s_____ of many, will appear a s_____ time, not to deal with sin but to s_____ those who are e_____ waiting for Him.

This verse is packed with information.

2. When Christ came the first time, what did He come to do?

   To "bear the s_____ of many."

3. This verse speaks of the inevitability of judgment for all mankind. When does that judgment occur?

   After we d_____.

There is no second chance for this; we can die only once. After that we must face judgment, but what type of judgment depends on our position in Christ.

4. What is the promise for those who are eagerly waiting for His Second Coming?

   He will s_____ them.

The Greek word for "save" here is *soteria*.[15] It connotes deliverance, preservation from danger. When He appears the second time, He will deliver us from danger, preserving us from the wrath to come and saving us out of the terrible days of the great tribulation. No wonder those who are alive and left will be eagerly waiting for Him.

---

[15] Zodhiates, *Hebrew-Greek Key*, 1676

5.   Read John 5:22–27. Answer the questions below. Who is our judge?

   a.   God the Father
   b.   God the Son
   c.   God the Holy Spirit

Who has given all judgment to the Son?

   a.   God the Father
   b.   God the Son
   c.   God the Holy Spirit

Jesus is our Judge! He is our Savior and our Judge, the Just and the Justifier, as Romans 3:26 explains.

6.   Believers have eternal life already at the moment of salvation, and after death, we do not come into judgment regarding salvation. (Praise God!) Instead we pass from…(John 5:21)

   a.   death to life
   b.   life to death.

The moment we die, we pass from death to life, eternal life, and we are assured of eternity with Him. That is when our *real* life begins.

7.   Who will be judged? Read Romans 14:10–12 and circle the correct answers.

   a.   Good people
   b.   Bad people
   c.   Lost people
   d.   Saved people
   e.   All the above

We will all be judged. We must all give an account to God. However, there are different judgments.

For believers, there is the judgment seat of Christ (2 Corinthians 5:6–10).

For the lost, there is the great white throne judgment (Revelation 20:11–15).

And there is a third judgment, it seems: the sheep and goat judgment (Matthew 25:31–46).

(This judgment is possibly for those who go through the day of the Lord, for those who experience salvation [sheep] and for those who remain lost [goats] during that time of wrath.

Their relationship to Christ will be evident in their compassion or lack thereof toward the least of these. Or this may be a picture, a composite, of both of the above judgments.)

First, let us examine the judgment seat of Christ. This is the judgment for believers, an accounting of our lives.

8. Read 2 Corinthians 5:6–10 and fill in the blanks.

    For we must a_____ appear before the j_____ seat of C_____, so that each one may r_____ what is d_____ for what he has done in the b_____, whether g_____ or e_____.

For those in Christ, judgment isn't about whether we go to heaven or hell. It's not about our salvation; our salvation and eternity are secure for those who have trusted Christ as Savior. As we read in John 5:24, we are actually already in eternal life, and our death just ushers us into that.

However, there will be an accounting. We must all appear there and account for and receive accordingly for that which we did while in the body. Our present-day actions have eternal consequences. How we live matters.

This is one of the verses that implies rewards in heaven; it does not say *what* we receive for the good done while in our bodies, but it indicates that something will be received. Again, how we live matters eternally.

There is another judgment, the great white throne, the judgment of the lost. This may be the judgment of those to whom Jesus referred in John 5:28–29 (the lost are also resurrected) for judgment.

9. Read Revelation 20:11–15. This is a most solemn ceremony. It takes one's breath away to simply read it. Where are the dead (unsaved) standing?

    Before "the great w_____ throne."

Imagine the scene. God is on His great white throne, so powerful and awesome that from His presence even earth and sky have fled. There is only God on His throne and the lost, who apparently have the audacity to stand before Him.

10. There are two types of books opened at this ceremony. What are they (Revelation 20:12)?

    a. The book of death
    b. The book of life
    c. The book of each one's works, what he or she had done

11. Now read closely. On what basis are the dead thrown into the lake of fire (Revelation 20:12–15)?

    a. On the basis of what they had done, their works
    b. On the basis of their name not being found in the book of life

Like the saved, the unsaved must give an account for what was done while in the body. But salvation, or lack thereof, is based on Christ alone. Those who stand before the great white throne of God, whose names are not found in the [Lamb's] book of life, will be thrown into the lake of fire, their judgment based on Christ alone.

Such knowledge should serve as an impetus like never before to share the good news of salvation in Him. May we be the beautiful feet by which someone hears the gospel and by faith believes (Romans 10:14–17).

Answer key: 5. b   7. e
              5. a   10. b, c
              6. a   11. b

CHAPTER 16

SEQUENCE OF EVENTS, PART 1: NEW TESTAMENT

Once again, to organize the layers of data you have obtained thus far, fill in the sequence line below and add to it the additional points of information listed below. This will serve as your cheat sheet of all the information we have mined in the New Testament (except for Revelation); it is a treasure.

Terms to add: the temple (implied, as rebuilt), rebellion/apostasy, removal of restrainer, and the resurrection/new body.

Tribulation	Great Tribulation	Day of the Lord

Birth pangs
False christs/prophets/be on guard
Wars, famines, earthquakes, pestilence
Restrainer removed
Abomination of desolation/man of lawlessness/son of
destruction in the holy place where he ought not be
Falling away/family betrayal/rebellion/apostasy
Temple (implied)
Hated for His Name/persecution/martydom
Words given by Holy Spirit
Jerusalem trampled/Gentiles
Jesus's survival information for Judea/concern for pregnant
Sun, moon, and stars affected
Great Tribulation cut short for elect
Second Coming of Christ
God's wrath on the earth
All earth tribes mourn or fear
No one knows the hour or day
Dead saints are resurrected/changed
Living elect are gathered or rescued/changed
One taken/other left

SUMMATION

Someday the wars, famines, plagues, pestilences, and earthquakes our world has always experienced will worsen—perhaps exponentially. We aren't privy to the events taking place in heaven that will precipitate this, but the final seven years of this age will someday (perhaps soon) begin. These increasingly intense birth pangs will signal that this present age is coming to a close.

A charismatic ruler will rise and make a covenant of supposed peace. Perhaps that covenant will involve rebuilding a temple or tabernacle on the Temple Mount—a feat of great consequence. Somehow, the sacrificial system will be reinstated. Though we as believers know sacrifices are no longer needed because Jesus was the perfect Lamb of God, there are religious Jews (who do not believe in Yeshua, Jesus, as their Messiah) who are ready to reinstitute the sacrificial system at any moment.

Then the leader, the Antichrist (man of lawlessness, son of destruction, abomination of desolation) will break that covenant after three and a half years. The divinely appointed restrainer will cease from holding him back, and he will be revealed. His charade of being someone who offers peace and safety will cease, and he will be revealed for who he really is, stopping the newly instituted sacrificial system and setting himself up in the temple, the holy place, where he ought not to be, as the abomination that makes it desolate, proclaiming himself to be God.

Many will be deceived. There will be a falling away, also known as "the apostasy." It seems that even people in the church, unsaved members, will turn on the true church, the believers. Martyrdom will ensue. True believers in some cases will be reported by their own family members. The great tribulation will be underway. This will precipitate history's greatest opportunity for believers to witness, being given their very words by the Holy Spirit, and the gospel will be proclaimed throughout the world. Jerusalem will be surrounded by armies, and people there will flee to the mountains to escape the Antichrist.

But we as believers must keep our gaze upward. For the church, for the true believers, redemption is near. The persecution and martyrdom will be limited. God "cuts short" or amputates the great tribulation. He turns out the lights in the heavens, and only His Shekinah, His glory, will light the sky as He comes in the clouds to rescue His church. He will return with the already-dead believers, resurrect their bodies to immortal perfection, and then gather up or rapture those still alive and left, also giving them new, perfect, immortal bodies—all in the blink of an eye.

Back on earth, the day of the Lord will have commenced. With Christ's return, after getting the church out of harm's way, the wrath of God will descend on planet earth. We will learn much more about this in the Old Testament and Revelation, in parts 2 and 3 of this study.

Let's go back in time now and study the Old Testament prophets. We will see that much of what they recorded has indeed already happened, but much of it is yet to be.

Amen, come Lord Jesus!

PART 2

THE OLD TESTAMENT PROPHECIES

In the Old Testament prophetic texts, we find the foundation and background for all we studied in the New Testament. As you know, many of the prophecies weren't completely fulfilled at the first coming of Christ; much of what the old prophets recorded is yet to be.

Therefore, reading them can be confusing because we understand something the prophets did not ... that there were to be two comings of the Messiah and that there would be an age for the church, the time between His comings. So it is often difficult for the current reader to know where the prophet is in time.

Many of the prophecies have been fulfilled already but not in the ultimate sense. We will see much of the already-but-not-yet paradigm. Many events they foretold have happened already, but they will happen again, usually in a more profound manner. For instance, Israel has experienced many days of the Lord—desolations, wars, dispersions, and captivities—but there is still coming an ultimate day.

Also, though obvious, we must remember that the Old Testament centers on Israel and the Jewish people. Other nations are mentioned only as they intersect with Israel. Therefore, as prophetic events are fulfilled, their consequences unfold like ripples in a pond. Jerusalem receives the heaviest impact, but the ripples flow to the rest of the world.

This examination of eschatology in the Old Testament is by no means exhaustive, so in keeping with the scope and purpose of the study, we have limited our examination to texts that deal explicitly with the end of this age. There is so much more to be found. Also, we will see a great deal of repetition. God knew we needed to read and hear things again and again to really remember them.

CHAPTER 17

ISAIAH

As Isaiah 1:1 says, it was written concerning Judah and Jerusalem during the reigns of four kings of Judah. It was written to a "sinful nation," who had "forsaken the Lord" and "despised the Holy One of Israel" (1:4). Like a piece of classical music, this anthology of oracles swings back and forth between portions of heavy, deserved judgment—the day of the Lord and joyful promises of a golden age—the restoration.

REGARDING THE LATTER DAYS

1. Read Isaiah 2:1–5. Answer the questions below.

   Have these events happened yet? _____

Taking these verses at face value (a "plain" hermeneutic), what will happen to the topography of the Temple Mount (Isaiah 2:2)?

   It "shall be l_____ up above the hills."

   c. The Jews
   d. The nation of Israel
   e. All the nations

3. Who will judge and decide disputes (2:4)?

   a. King David
   b. The Lord

4. What will be made into plowshares and pruning hooks—think of agricultural, peaceful tools (2:4)?

   S_____ and s_____

5. What do you think these verses seem to be describing?

   a. A future of peace on earth for all peoples, with the Lord as King and Judge, an earthly reign.
   b. The eternal state, heaven
   c. The new heavens and the new earth

The authors would circle "a" because we believe in a literal reign of Christ on planet earth (Revelation 20). However, many learned scholars would circle "b" or "c." In these matters, the essential truth is that our God reigns.

Pause and praise Him that there is coming a day of peace when all nations will desire the ways of the Lord.

Answer Key: 2. c   3. b   5. ?

REGARDING THE PROMISED GOLDEN AGE

Though the Old Testament never mentions a one-thousand-year reign or millennium, there is a pervasive idea of a golden, peaceful age on planet earth after this present age has passed.

1. Read the familiar verses of Isaiah 9:6–7. What punctuation separates His first and second coming in these verses? _____
   That semicolon represents the entire church age. The Child has been born, the Son has been given, but peace has not increased, and human government is not upon His shoulders … yet.

2. Read Isaiah 11:1–9. There is a description of peace here that doesn't yet exist, where natural enemies dwell happily together. Fill in the blanks below (11:6–8).

   Wolf and l____
   Leopard and young g_____
   Lion and fattened _____
   Nursing child and c_____

3. How will this be possible (11:9)? Fill in the blanks.

"...for the earth [apparently even the animals] shall be f_____ of the k_____ of the Lord"

REGARDING THE DAY OF THE LORD

There are approximately fifty references to the day of the Lord in Isaiah. Get out your *Strong's Concordance* or Bible app and look them up. You will repeatedly see that this day is described as a day like no other, a time when God will intervene in punishment and wrath (what we deserve), followed by restoration and grace (what we have in Christ). Throughout Israel's history, there have been many days of the Lord, but there is coming a time such has never been seen before.

1. Read Isaiah 2:10–12 and 2:17–22. Read Revelation 6:12–16 and compare these verses. When the day comes, how will the lofty, proud, and haughty respond?

   a. They will be happy, comfortable, and smug.
   b. They will repent.
   c. They will hide in terror in the caves and rocks and holes in the ground.

Of what or whom are they so afraid (Isaiah 2:21)?

   The t_____ of the Lord.
   The s_____ of His majesty.
   And (Revelation 6:16) "the w_____ of the Lamb."

The day of the Lord is the time of His wrath, splendor, and majesty. No little baby in a manger this time; He is coming in His fully revealed glory, bringing with Him the consequences for having rejected His free gift of grace.

2. Read Isaiah 13:6–13. What kind of day is the day of the Lord (13:8–9)?

   a. Bright and sunny
   b. Cruel with wrath and fierce anger
   c. A day like any other
   d. A day of dismay, agony, and anguish

3. What is the purpose of the day of the Lord (13:9)?

   To make the l_____ a desolation and to d_____ its s_____ from it.

Here we see a description of the horror of the day of the Lord. Much has happened in Israel's history, but there is much in these verses that hasn't happened in the ultimate sense yet.

4. Read Isaiah 13:10–13 and fill in the blanks. What heavenly bodies are affected *before* the day of the Lord?

   S_____, m_____ and s_____.

5. Recall that Jesus told us that immediately after the terrible tribulation and before His return, the sun, moon, and stars will be affected and darkened (Matthew 24:29–31). We see it also in Acts.

Read Acts 2:20 and fill in the blanks.

   The sun shall be turned to darkness and the moon to blood b_____ the day of the Lord comes.

6. And in Revelation 6:12–14. Fill in the blanks.

   The sun became b_____ as sackcloth, the full moon became like b_____, and the stars of the sky f_____.

Throughout His Word, we see that God darkens His creation to herald the coming of His day, His return in glory, bringing His wrath on the sinful world.

Remember, though, we believers aren't appointed or destined to be objects of His wrath. When we trusted Christ, He bore the wrath for us (1 Thessalonians 5:9).

Immediately after the great tribulation has run its course, God turns out the lights. The terrible tribulation is "cut short" by this upheaval of the heavenly bodies to herald the beginning of the day of the Lord, and His first order of business is to rescue His people.

7. Number the following terms in the order in which they will occur:

   - Sun, moon, and stars affected
   - Haughty and proud hiding in terror
   - Terrible tribulation
   - Day of the Lord
   - Gathering the elect
   - Christ's return

Answers

1. Terrible tribulation
2. Sun, moon, and stars affected
3. Haughty and proud hide in terror
4. Christ's return

5. Gathering of believers
6. Day of the Lord

As we learned in the New Testament study and as we will see throughout this Old Testament portion, when the Lord returns and begins His day, the world will be terrifying and chaotic. He will rescue His own out of that terrible distress, but for the lost, conditions will become unimaginably worse, like something from a science fiction movie. Understanding this fact serves to spur us on to share the gospel, because it is only in Christ that anyone can be saved.

Answer Key: 1. C   2. B, d

REGARDING THE LAND AND GOD'S HEART FOR ISRAEL

Israel is a unique land, and she will play a unique role in the latter days. That tiny, narrow strip acts as a land bridge between three continents, and God has had His hand on her from the beginning of time. So has Satan. God chose Israel to be the land where His Son would be born and the Jews to be His lineage. No wonder Satan hates her and her people with a particular vehemence.

Throughout history, Jews have been enslaved, held captive, banished, and dispersed throughout the world. The major ancient empires—Egypt, Assyria, Babylon, Media-Persia, Greece, and Rome—all held a particular hatred for Israel, because Satan did and still does. Though the enemy has tried repeatedly to destroy Israel and the Jews, there have always been survivors, known as "the remnant." A few always remained in the land, but many throughout history were displaced outside of Israel. The resulting diaspora placed many Jews throughout Europe, Africa, Asia, Russia, and later the United States.

Then in the late 1800s and early 1900s, the Zionist movement gathered momentum to re-establish a homeland for the Jew.[16] When Israel was recognized as a nation again on May 14, 1948, it was the first time in almost two thousand years. The stage was set for Jewish people to return to their homeland. Isaiah prophesied this return.

8. Read Isaiah 10:20–23. Who will return to the mighty God (10:21)?

    A r_____ will return, the r_____ of Jacob (Israel).

9. Read Isaiah 37:31–32. What is the remnant called?

    A band of s_____.

10. Read Isaiah 11:11–12. From where will He assemble the banished and dispersed of Israel (11:12)?

    From the f_____ corners of the e_____.

11. Read Isaiah 14:1–2. Where will the Lord set them (14:1)?

    In their own l_____.

12. Read Isaiah 60:20–21. How long will they possess the land (60:21)?

    F_____.

---

[16] Wikipedia, s.v. "History of Zionism." Last edited April, 2020 http:/en.wikipedia.org/History of Zionism

The return of the Jewish people to Israel after the Babylonian captivity was the near future, the already-but-not-yet fulfillment of many of these passages in Isaiah. We are now seeing in our lifetime the distant-future fulfillment as thousands of Jews are returning to Israel, making Aliyah. At the time of this writing, Prime Minister Benjamin Netanyahu encourages them that Judea and Samaria is their homeland and that the law of return, enacted by Israel's Knesset in 1950,[17] gives them rights and citizenship. God's promises to Israel are being fulfilled in our lifetime, and the promise of *forever* will one day be fulfilled.

13. Read Isaiah 49:6, 13–16, 22–23, 26. Zion felt the Lord had forgotten them. Can He? _____

14. Read Isaiah 51:2–3, 11, 16. What will Zion's desert become like?

    The g_____ of the Lord.

15. Read Isaiah 44:21. Will God forget Israel?_____

16. Read Isaiah 62:1–4, 11–12. As you read through all the above verses, how do you think God feels about Israel?

    a. He is finished with her.
    b. He has replaced her with the church.
    c. He loves her with an everlasting, covenant-keeping love. He made promises to her He will keep.

He loves her with an everlasting, covenant-keeping love. Presently, Israel is largely an unregenerate nation. There are many religious people there, but if they don't have a saving faith in Yeshua, the Messiah, they are lost. Israel and the Jewish people must be saved, just as anyone is, by grace alone through faith in Christ alone. No one can come to the Father except through Jesus (John 14:6). But clearly Israel has a unique place in God's plan, and He loves her. As we learned in the New Testament portion, and as we will see in Revelation, she plays a prominent role in the unfolding of the end of this age.

---

[17] The Jewish Agency for Israel, https://www.google.com/jewishagency.org.

FINALLY, REGARDING THE NEW HEAVENS AND THE NEW EARTH

Before we leave the wonderful book of Isaiah, read Isaiah 65:17–25 *aloud*.

The new heavens and the new earth. Whether we view this as a description of the millennium on planet earth, newly created heavens and earth, or simply the beautiful eternal state, there is the assured promise of His peace and presence. There will be no more weeping or distress; there will be peaceful productivity and joy forevermore. God Himself will rejoice with us in the new Jerusalem. We have so much to look forward to.

Answers: 1. c
              2. b, d
            16. c

CHAPTER 18

JEREMIAH

Jeremiah was a priest and prophet during the reigns of the last kings of Judah and the beginning of the Babylonian captivity. Jeremiah was often called the weeping prophet; his heart was broken over his people's apostate condition. He was faithful. He called them to repentance hundreds of times but apparently had only two confirmed converts.

The day of the Lord theme is dominant in Jeremiah. Repeatedly he wrote of God's coming judgment and wrath on His people as a consequence of their persistent covenant infidelity. God used it to remove the people from the land, discipline them, end their idolatry, allow the land her Sabbath rest, and ultimately restore them back in the land of Israel.

1. Read Jeremiah 25:1–13 and fill in the blanks. How long was the Babylonian captivity to last (25:11–12)?

   _____years.

2. Why did God have them go into captivity (25:8)?

   Because you have not o_____ my words.

And just as the Babylonian captivity and the anger of the Lord had a limited time frame, so will the ultimate day of the Lord (though we don't know the duration of the day of the Lord); after His wrath, restoration comes for those who turn to Him.

3. Ultimately, how long has the Lord given Israel the land (25:5)?

   F_____.

4. Read Jeremiah 30:1–3, 10–11, 18.

What will God do to the nations among whom He scattered Jacob (Israel) (v. 11)?

Make a f_____ e_____.

And where shall the city be rebuilt (30:18)?

On its m_____ … where it used to be.

In these verses and so many others, we see that it happened already but not yet. Jacob (Israel) did return from the Babylonian captivity, and things were quieter and somewhat easier (v. 10), and Jerusalem and the temple were rebuilt, but the temple was again destroyed, and Israel has since never enjoyed a truly lasting peace. These prophecies were fulfilled but not ultimately and forever—not yet.

5. Read Jeremiah 31:1–3. With what type of love does God love all Israel?

E_____.

6. Read 31:8–9. From where will He gather the remnant of Israel?

From the n_____ … from the f_____ parts of the e_____.

Already, thousands of Jews have returned to Israel from Russia and Europe, north of Israel.

7. Read 31:31–36 and write a brief paragraph to answer the questions below.
   Based on reading these few verses, how do you think God feels about the land and the people of Israel? All His promises were fulfilled in Christ, but has God replaced Israel? How long does it seem that God will love Israel? How long will she be a nation before Him?

_____

_____

_____

_____

God keeps promises. Someday on some glorious day, there will be neither Jew nor Gentile (Galatians 3:28). There will just be believers, His sons and daughters.

CHAPTER 19

LAMENTATIONS

Lamentations, a lament, is a profound and sorrowful little book written by an eyewitness of the destruction of Jerusalem and the temple, and the Babylonian captivity. As such, its writer, probably Jeremiah, lived through a kind of day of the Lord. There is no distant-future prophecy to be found here, but the depiction of a day of the Lord gives us much to ponder.

1. Read Lamentations 4:8–11 to comprehend the horrors of the consequences of sin. To what did the Lord give full vent (4:11)?

   His w_____.

And yet in this book we read one of the most beautiful assertions of His promise-keeping love.

2. Read Lamentations 3:22–24. You may want to sing it to Him. When does the steadfast love of the Lord cease?

   N_____.

When do His mercies come to an end?

   N_____.

What are they every morning?

   N_____.

CHAPTER 20

EZEKIEL

Ezekiel was written to Judah, the people of the southern kingdom of Israel, during their Babylonian exile and captivity. Jeremiah may have been Ezekiel's mentor. Like Isaiah and Jeremiah, the book is a message of God's uncompromising judgment and promise of restoration for His name's sake, not because it is deserved but because of His grace and for the glory of His name. The day of the Lord's wrath is a major theme with the particular emphasis that it will come on Israel because of her abominations.

1. Read Ezekiel 1:4–29.

The book opens with Ezekiel's powerful vision of the throne room of heaven. We can get so caught up in the wheels and wings and impossible movement of the four living creatures that we miss the indescribable majesty of God in verses 26–27. Herein the theme for the book is set—the holiness of God contrasted with the sins of His people. Yet He loves them.

Draw a little sketch of what you read in verses 26–27. Imagine it.

2. Read Ezekiel 36:22–28. (This has been called the key passage of the book of Ezekiel.) For whose sake does God bring Israel back to the land (36:22)?

   a. God's and His holy name
   b. Israel's
   c. Future generations

For the sake of His holy name, God will vindicate His holiness before the eyes of the nations through the nation of Israel. He will remove their [Israel's] heart of stone so they may dwell in the land He gave their fathers.

3. How will the people of Israel finally be able to walk in His statutes?

    d. They will cleanse themselves.
    e. They will work hard to obey.
    f. They will reinstitute sacrifices.
    g. He will put His Spirit in them.

God assures them that they will by His Spirit, which He will place in them, be able to walk in His ways.

4. Read 36:33–35 and fill in the blanks. When they again dwell in their land, what will people say it is like (36:35)?

The g_____ of E_____.

Already, as one travels through the land of Israel, the cultivation, irrigation, and beauty are amazing, particularly their cherry tomatoes. As we saw on a recent trip to Israel, what had been a malaria-infested swamp about one hundred years ago is now blooming and beautiful. Because of Israeli technology, desalination of the Mediterranean, their irrigation systems, and a strong work ethic, Israel is truly blooming.

THE VALLEY OF DRY BONES

God may have depicted this rejuvenation of Israel in a unique vision He gave Ezekiel.

5. Read all chapter 37. Just imagine what Ezekiel saw and heard. Fill in the blanks.

What was the sound he heard (37:7)?

R_____ as the dry b_____ came together.

6. What do the dry bones that came alive represent (37:11)?

The w_____ house of I_____.

Many scholars believe we saw this event come to pass in recent history. On May 14, 1948, after almost two thousand years of being out of her homeland, the nation of Israel came alive and was *born in one day* (Isaiah 66:8). The dry bones lived. All the prophesied events of the latter days regarding the nation of Israel became possible because of her rebirth. We could well be living in the most exciting era of human history.

GOG AND MAGOG

Before leaving this prophet, we must turn our attention to two more subjects unique to Ezekiel—Gog and Magog, and the vision of a new temple.

Gog and Magog are two names or terms often mentioned when end-times are discussed, and novelists and movie producers enjoy making much of them. However, with the exception of a Magog mentioned as a descendant of Japheth (1 Chronicles 1:5) and a Gog being mentioned as a descendant of Reuben (1 Chronicles 5:4), these are the only places where we read of these names in the Old Testament. They aren't mentioned again until Revelation 20:7–9, when they are destroyed at the very end of the age, "when the thousand years are ended … and fire … from heaven … consumed them."

7. Read Ezekiel 38–39. Draw lines to match the following (38:1):

   Gog is a   land
   Magog is a   man, prince of Meshech and Tubal

8. When Israel is dwelling securely, Gog will come with a mighty army from which direction? Circle the correct response (38:15).

   East   North   South   West

Jews have been returning to Israel predominantly from the north, and now we see that this mighty army invades … from the north.

9. Who fights Gog and wins (Ezekiel 38:18–23)?

   a. God
   b. Israel

10. Who brings them against the people of Israel (38:14–16)?

    a. God
    b. Satan
    c. Magog

11. Why does God do this (38:16)?

    That the n_____ may know Me.

Remember, God's purpose in demonstrating His steadfast love, mercy, and grace to Israel was so the nations would know Him. Just as He used Babylon and other nations *against* Israel for His glory, He will use Gog in the last days.

Chapters 38–39 of Ezekiel speak much of what we will see in Revelation. Here we read of huge armies coming against Israel, an earthquake that changes the topography of the land, birds of prey that eat the flesh of the hordes that come against Israel, and finally the true peace and security God promised as He poured His Spirit on the house of Israel.

From Revelation 20, it would appear that the battle described happens *after* the one-thousand-year period to, in essence, sop up all the nonbelievers born during that golden age. However, many scholars associate this battle of Gog and Magog with the sixth bowl of Revelation 16:12–16 and 19:18–21 and the battle of Armageddon because of the bird feast.

Regardless of when, in the end God will use an army from the north to come against Israel when she is at peace, and He will destroy them for His glory. All the nations *will know* He is God.

EZEKIEL'S BLUEPRINT FOR A TEMPLE

Now we come to a very fascinating portion of scripture. The final nine chapters of Ezekiel, a great deal of text, are given to a description and blueprint for a temple that hasn't yet been built. Is this a literal temple, a metaphor, the tribulation temple, the millennial temple, or the heavenly temple?

The temple described is huge, with very detailed measurements, descriptions of the architecture and design, as well as rules for priests, sacrifices, and festivals. God gives Ezekiel a tour throughout the entire complex.

When Ezekiel had last seen the temple, God transported him from Babylon to Jerusalem to watch as the Shekinah, the glory of God, departed from the first temple (Ezekiel 10:18–19). The glory slowly departed from above the cherubim, over the outer court, and through the East Gate due to the abominable sin of the people. At this point in the narrative, he is privileged to watch as the glory of God returned and filled this new temple.

12. Read Ezekiel 43:1–9. From which direction does God's glory return?

    a. North
    b. South
    c. East
    d. West

The glory of God actually already came and strode into the temple from the east—in Jesus. But they knew Him not, and He had to chase the money changers from His Father's house.

13. The next time the glory of God returns, how long will He dwell in the midst of His people, Israel (Ezekiel 43:7)?

    F_____.

14. How long will His people dwell there (Ezekiel 37:25)?

    F_____.

15. How long will His sanctuary be in their midst (Ezekiel 37:26–28)?

    F_____.

As we read the last verses of Ezekiel, God may be giving us a preview of what John saw in Revelation 21:10–27, the New Jerusalem.

16. Read Ezekiel 48:35. What is the name of the city from that time on?

   The LORD is T_____.

As He promised, the Lord will forevermore be in the midst of His people. Ezekiel closes with this wonderful promise, the ultimate *rest of the story*.

Answer Key:

   2. a
   3. g
   8. a
   9. a
   11. c

CHAPTER 21

DANIEL

The book of Daniel has more specific end-time information than all the other prophets. Interestingly, the book is sealed (Daniel 12:4, 9) until the time of the end. Perhaps this book will not be fully understood until the latter days, at which time it will make perfect sense, maybe just as the events unfold.

So don't be discouraged if Daniel is difficult. We will just walk through it, learn what it says, and discover what we can. Who knows? If it all starts to make perfect sense, maybe the time of the end is closer than we think.

We will examine only portions specifically pertaining to the time of the end.

DANIEL 2

Read Daniel 2:31–45.

Here we see world history depicted in a statue. You will recall that after Daniel's deportation from Israel to Babylon, King Nebuchadnezzar had a dream and required his wise men not only to tell him his dream but also to interpret it under penalty of death. Daniel intervened and declared that only God could reveal the dream and its meaning, and He does. Draw the statue and label its materials (2:31–45).

1. What struck the statue (2:34)?

    A s_____.

2. What part of the statue did the stone strike?

    The f_____.

3. What happened to the whole statue when the stone struck the feet (2:35)?

    It "became like c_____ ... and not a t_____ of them could be f_____."

4. When this stone struck the feet, the whole thing came tumbling down and ceased to exist. What happened to the stone (2:35)?

    It "became a g_____ m_____ and f_____ the whole earth."

5. Who or what do you think the stone is?

    a. The kingdom of God
    b. The Lord Jesus Christ

You really can't go wrong with your answer. He reigns and reduces all other kingdoms to chaff.

6. Scholars are in general agreement as to the historical kingdoms the statue represented. Go back to your sketch of the statue and label the kingdoms represented.

    Head of gold—Babylon
    Chest and arms of silver—Medo-Persian empire
    Belly and thighs of bronze—Greece
    Legs of iron—Rome

7. Read Daniel 2:41–45. What are the feet and toes made of (2:41)?

    Partly of potters c_____ and partly of i_____.

As far as we know, this is a kingdom that as yet isn't identifiable in history.

8. What type of kingdom does this mixing of material result in? Circle all that apply.

united	admixture
divided	soft
cohesive	partly brittle
peaceful	unable to hold together
partly strong	firm

When visualizing this statue, we see historical kingdoms down through the legs, but the feet and toes are different. During the days of the kings represented by those weird toes, God does something He has never done before.

9. What will God do during the days of those presumably ten (the ten toes) kings (Daniel 2:44–45)?

    God will "set up a k_____ that will n_____ be d_____."

10. How long does this kingdom last?

    F_____.

Since we know God will set up His kingdom during the days of that mixed, divided, partly strong, partly brittle, as-yet-unknown ten nations or kings or kingdoms, we know it will be the *last* world power before God's kingdom. When that particular kingdom comes on the stage of human history, God will set up His own Kingdom which will never be destroyed.

We must jump ahead for a moment to see this fulfilled in Revelation.

11. Read Revelation 17:12–14. How many kings join with the beast (Antichrist) to destroy the prostitute Babylon and make war with the Lamb?

    _____

Now, it is important to note that when the stone destroys the whole statue, the kingdoms are all still in existence. Though they are no longer world powers, they did *not* cease to exit. We know them today as the following:

Iraq—Babylon
Iran—Persia
Syria—Grecian Empire
Europe and the Middle East—Rome

We can only speculate as to what the non-cohesive toe nations will be, but we know that when they do join together briefly, they will comprise the kingdom of the Antichrist. When the Lord Jesus destroys it, all the others will fall.

DANIEL 7

Sometime later, in chapter 7, Daniel had a dream, and in it those four kingdoms of chapter 2 were depicted as beasts.

12. Read Daniel 7:1–6. Try to draw the first three beasts and any action they take.

Again, there is general scholarly agreement as to what these beasts represent.

The lion whose wings are plucked and made to stand represents Babylon and Nebuchadnezzar's humbling followed by his reinstatement.

The bear on its side with three ribs represents the Medo-Persian empire.

The leopard with four wings represents Alexander the Great, the Greek empire, which was eventually divided between four generals.

Again, we must jump to Revelation to see the comparison.

13. Read Revelation 13:1–2 for the fulfillment of this dream. What is the beast (Antichrist) like?

"A l_____ … a b_____ and … l_____," the same beasts Daniel saw. In history, these kingdoms had an unholy hatred for the nation of Israel, just as the Antichrist will.

It was the fourth beast in Daniel's dream that he described as terrifying, dreadful, and different. This beast had ten horns and cannot be compared to any beast Daniel ever saw.

14. Read Daniel 7:7–8. Draw this beast in the two frames below, depicting the actions of the horns before and after the eleventh (little) horn emerges.

Before—with ten horns   After—when the little horn arises

15. Read Daniel 7:19–22. Like us, Daniel desired to know more about the fourth beast. What did the little horn do until the Ancient of Days intervened?

   This horn made w_____ with the s_____ and prevailed over them.

Are you beginning to form an opinion as to who this little horn represents?

16. Read Daniel 7:23–25 closely. Out of which kingdom do the ten horns rise?

   a. The first
   b. The second
   c. The third
   d. The fourth

17. What empire does the fourth kingdom probably represent in both the statue of chapter 2 and the beasts of chapter 7? Circle one.

   a. Babylon
   b. Media/Persia
   c. Greece
   d. Rome

18. When does another horn, the eleventh, rise?

   a. Before the fourth kingdom
   b. After the fourth kingdom

The eleventh horn (king) arises from among the ten. The ten arose from the fourth kingdom that devoured the whole earth. Rome was such a kingdom. It encompassed most of the known world when it was in power. Though all this is the future to Daniel, he was speaking also of ten kings and another different king, who will emerge in the (to him) *very* distant future.

Remember, Rome doesn't exist as an empire today, but all the countries it encompassed still do … most of Europe and the Middle East. This *little* horn (king) arises from among the other ten. The other ten arise from the old Roman Empire. This *little* horn is different; it seems greater than the other ten (7:20) and uproots three of them (7:24).

19. Read Daniel 7:25. What will this little horn do? Fill in the blanks.

   "He shall speak words a_____ the Most High" and even audaciously thinks he can change the times and the law, probably because the time has been appointed for his end. He will "w_____ o_____" or oppress the

saints, and they will indeed be given to him for "a t_____, t_____
and half a t_____."

It seems that Daniel was given a great deal of specific information very long ago about a character now known as the Antichrist. From Daniel, we learn his origin, his character, and how long he is allowed to wield his power.

20. Read Revelation 13:5–8; it practically quotes the above passage. How long is a time, times, and half a time?

_____ months (or three and a half years).

Dear brothers and sisters, though the saints are given to this horn (king), the Antichrist, this is for a limited, appointed, prescribed, and previously set time.

Now, before we leave chapter 7, we must backtrack to a glorious *meanwhile*. While Daniel watches as this horrific beast comes into power, he is taken to see the throne room of heaven.

21. Read Daniel 7:9–11 aloud. Court was called into session. What happened to the beast (7:11)?

The beast was k_____.

While in the throne room of heaven, we get to skip to the end and see that the demise of the beast is a sure thing.

22. Read Daniel 7:16–18. Even Daniel was alarmed by all he had seen, and he needed reassurance. What was he told regarding the saints of the Most High (7:18)?

They "possess the kingdom f_____, f_____ and e_____."

Days (7:13–14)?

_____

24. How long is His kingdom and dominion?

E_____.

Jesus, the Son of Man, is the King of glory, and He will come on the clouds of heaven, and His dominion is everlasting.

25. Place the following events in numerical order to help summarize the information found in Daniel 7.

    A. Ten horns will rise from the fourth kingdom.
    B. He (the little horn) shall speak against the Most High and wear out the saints.
    C. The saints will be given to him for a time, times, and half a time (three and a half years); he will want to change the times because they determine his set end.
    D. An everlasting kingdom will be given to the saints.
    E. His kingdom will be destroyed.
    F. A fourth kingdom with iron teeth devours, breaks, and stomps (the earth).
    G. Another little (perhaps previously insignificant individual) horn (king) arises from the ten and uproots three of the others

Answer key: 5. a, b
              16. d
              17. d
              18. b
              24. F A G B C E D

DANIEL 8

Two years later, in chapter 8, Daniel had a vision of a ram and a goat. The vision is extremely detailed, and the angel Gabriel was told to make Daniel understand it. Gabriel explained some very specific information about two future (to Daniel) kingdoms.

26. Read Daniel 8:19–22. Who do the two horns of the ram represent?

    K_____ of M_____ and P_____.

27. Who does the goat represent?

    King of G_____.

We know Alexander the Great from our history books. After conquering much of the known world, he died at age thirty-three, and his kingdom was divided among four generals.[18] Daniel was told precise information regarding events that would take place about three hundred years later. What an omniscient God we serve!

Particular information is given regarding one of these four generals (horns).

---

[18] *The ESV Study Bible*. 2008, Crossway Bibles, study notes, 1605

28. Read Daniel 8:23–27.

This is a description of Antiochus Epiphanes, the eighth king of the Seleucid Empire, one of the four from the division of the Greek empire after Alexander's death. History tells us he was a tyrant who hated the Jews, burning the scriptures and crucifying thousands, actually hanging circumcised infants around their mother's necks. He defiled the temple and sacrificed a pig to a statue of Zeus, bearing his own face.[19] Using an unclean animal to worship a false god polluted and desolated the temple. It was an abomination to the Jews, an abomination that desolated their holy temple. The faithful Maccabees rebelled, and the temple was cleansed and restored to its rightful state, an event now celebrated as Hanukkah. All this took place during the four hundred so-called silent years, that period of history between the last prophet Malachi and the first advent of Christ.[20] No wonder poor Daniel lay sick for days (8:27). He saw the near *and* distant future, and he was appalled.

You may be wondering, *What does chapter 8 have to do with end-times? All the events of chapter 8 are now history; they happened before Christ's first coming.* True, they have happened, and they will happen again. As Gabriel told Daniel, the vision he had seen referred to the "time of the end" (8:17); and Jesus, when quoting Daniel in Matthew 24, referred to the abomination of desolation as something yet to take place.

Antiochus Epiphanes is what scholars refer to as a type, an individual with certain attributes or characteristics that prefigure one who is coming.[21] There were many types of Christ like Isaac and Boaz. The Antichrist also has a type … Antiochus Epiphanes.

It's important to note that the little horn of chapter 8 is *not* the same little horn of chapter 7. This can be confusing, but they arise from different kingdoms at different times. Antiochus Epiphanes rose before Christ's first coming, and the beast horn will rise in association with the events of Christ's Second Coming. They also rise from different kingdoms.

Antiochus Epiphanes serves to foreshadow the future Antichrist. He was in Daniel's near future, arising from the Grecian empire. Antichrist was in his distant future and will rise from the unknown future empire that is an admixture of iron and clay feet and toes, the empire that is associated with the indescribable beast, the ancient Roman Empire (although the Roman Empire did ultimately encompass most of the Grecian empire).

DANIEL 9

In chapter 9 we come to the seventy weeks or the seventieth week of the book of Daniel, an outline of eschatological events framed in time.

---

[19] Kevin Howard and Marvin Rosenthal, *The Feasts of the Lord* (Orlando: Zion's Hope, 1997), 163
[20] Howard and Rosenthal, *Feasts of the Lord*, 164 & 165
[21] *The ESV Study Bible, study notes*, 1605

Jeremiah prophesied the duration of the Babylonian captivity. Daniel, reading that prophecy while he was *in* Babylon, realized that the seventy years were almost complete. He prayed fervently, confessing the sins of his people. While doing so, Gabriel came to him in "swift flight" to give him understanding because he, Daniel, was "greatly loved" (9:21–23).

Daniel pled for his people because of God's mercy, for the sake of His name and for the people called by His name. In response to this, he was told of God's ultimate plan for His people and their restoration. He was told there was a prescribed amount of time to accomplish six events.

29. Read 9:24 and list the six events.

    a.

    b.

    c.

    d.

    e.

    f.

Answers: finish the transgression, put an end to sin, atone for iniquity, bring in everlasting righteousness, seal both the vision and prophecy, and anoint the most holy place.

30. Now consider the list you compiled from Daniel 9:24 and circle those you think have already been accomplished.

We know sin was atoned for on the cross (c) and that we have the complete cannon of vision and prophecy (e), but the others may not have been completely fulfilled yet. In Christ, *all* has been fulfilled, but the actualization of that is yet to come.

31. Read 9:25–26. The allocated time to accomplish all this is "70 weeks" or 490 years. In this context, a week equals seven years. (See Leviticus 25:8 for a week equaling seven years.)

Two chunks of time are mentioned. Let's do the math.

    7 weeks = (7 x 7 years) = _____ years
    62 weeks = (62 x 7 years) =_____ years
    434 years + 49 years =_____years

From the decree (and we can't be certain about which decree; was it Cyrus's in Ezra 1:2 or Artaxerxes's in Ezra 7:12?) to rebuild Jerusalem in a very troubled time (Israel no longer had a king) until the Anointed One (Messiah) was crucified, there were to be a total of 483 years. Seventy weeks of years would be 490 years.

Now that leaves one more week (of years). *There is one more seven-year period needed to complete the allocated seventy sevens.* Thus, we have *the seventieth* week. We have been living between the sixty-ninth and seventieth week since the death, burial, and resurrection of Christ.

The last seven years, the seventieth week, will accomplish the completion of the list we wrote above. Transgression will be finished, sin will end, the most holy place will be anointed, and everlasting righteousness will be ushered in.

To be biblically correct in our terminology, we must refer to the last seven years of this age as "the seventieth week of Daniel" or "Daniel's seventieth week." To call the last seven years of this age "the tribulation" or "great tribulation" is biblically erroneous because the great tribulation within that seven years is cut short, but the seventieth week isn't, nor can it be. The seventieth week entails more than just the tribulation and great tribulation. It also entails the day of the Lord.

In fact, only Daniel mentioned a seven-year time period associated with the latter days. Revelation always deals with three and a half years, forty-two months, or 1,260 days—the last half of the seventieth week.

The sixty-nine weeks take Israel from their return after the Babylonian captivity through the rebuilding of Jerusalem and the temple (that's probably why the forty-nine years are distinguished from the rest) up to the crucifixion of Christ, when the Anointed One was cut off (9:26). Then it is as though God pushed the "pause" or "hold" button. Israel and the Jewish people continue to exist and be greatly loved by God, but as a nation, for the most part they have not recognized Yeshua, Jesus, as their Messiah. With the resurrection and ascension of Christ, the church was born, and the church age began.

As far as heavenly time is concerned, we are living between the sixty-ninth and seventieth weeks, and we have been for almost two thousand years. The "pause" button remains pressed. Someday the Lamb will open the first seal on the scroll in heaven, and the last seven years of the seventy weeks will begin to bring this phase of human history to a close.

32. Read Daniel 9:26–27. In addition to the ESV, read these verses in several translations, particularly the NIV. This is a very difficult passage to comprehend and was even difficult for translators to translate, but let's try to *rightly divide the word* and break it into small pieces.

Who destroys the city and the sanctuary (9:26)?

   a. The prince who is to come
   b. The people of the prince who is to come

From your knowledge of history, what people destroyed the temple and Jerusalem in AD 70?

R_____.

Therefore, they, the ancient Roman Empire, are the people from whom the prince (Antichrist) is to come.

Recall the legs of iron followed by the feet and toes of iron mixed with clay (Daniel 2). Recall the horrible iron-toothed beast with the little horn rising from it (Daniel 7).

What kingdom did they both represent?

R_____.

In both images, Rome is represented with a future king and kingdom emerging from it. Also, remember that the ancient Roman Empire encompassed much of what today are Europe and the Middle East. This prince can come from any of those areas. A strong case could be made that he will come from the Seleucid region of the Grecian Empire because Antiochus Epiphanes did. Geographically this land was encompassed by the Roman Empire and is present-day Syria, Iraq, Iran, and Turkey.[22]

33. Read Daniel 9:26. What is the nearest antecedent and descriptive phrase to the pronoun "he" in Daniel 9:27?

The p_____ who i____ t____ c_____.

This prince, who is to come from the old Roman Empire, will make a strong covenant with many for one week, the last week of the seventy, the final seven years of this present age.

The Antichrist will make a strong (possibly convincing, promise-laden) agreement for seven years, presumably with the nation of Israel. Throughout history, Israel has longed for peace, and it has cost her dearly. In our lifetime she has given away chunks of her land for a peace that has not been realized. The covenant into which they enter with this prince will have much to do with a guarantee of peace and safety, but he will break that agreement halfway through the seven years, putting an end to sacrifice and offering (Daniel 9:27; 2 Thessalonians 2:3-4).

Since there is presently no sacrificial system in place and he puts an end to the sacrifices, we can assume they will have been resumed sometime during the first half of the seven years or even before.

---

[22] Paul H. Wright, *Rose Then and Now: Bible Map Atlas* (Carta, Jerusalem: Bristol Works, Rose Publishing, 2008),259

At the time of this writing, there are religious Jewish groups in Jerusalem that await the opportunity to rebuild the temple on the Temple Mount and reinstitute the sacrificial system. We visited the Temple Institute in the Jewish Quarter of the Old City in Jerusalem and saw that the furnishings are made, the altar for sacrifices built, and the vestments for the priests fashioned. It is easy to imagine without too much speculation that the strong covenant could involve their ability to reinstate sacrifices for a time. But three and a half years into the agreement, the prince will reveal himself for who he is, demand worship, put an end to their sacrifices, place himself in the temple, and proclaim himself to be God (2 Thessalonians 2:4).

At this point, in the middle of the seventieth week, the Antichrist *is* the abomination that desolates the temple (Matthew 24:15). He will be fully empowered by Satan, who has at that point been cast to earth and is furiously making war on those who hold to Jesus because he knows his time is short (Revelation 12:12–17).

34. What kind of end is poured out on the desolator (Daniel 9:27)?

    The d_____ end.

We can rest assured in Christ. All this is under God's control. He is sovereign. Desolations and wars are decreed, and so is the end of Satan and his Antichrist.

DANIEL 10–12

Read Daniel 10. Chapters 10–12 are a single vision. In chapter 10, the fascinating scene is depicted. Daniel was on the banks of the T_____ River (10:4). Remember, he was in Babylonia the entire time he was recording this book. An angel reassured him again that he was greatly loved and that his prayers had been heard. The vision he had there on the banks of the Tigris helped him understand what would happen to his people in the latter days (10:14).

His vision gives us insight into the activity and relationships of angels. We see their geographical assignments and their dealings with the demons, the princes of Persia and Greece, who apparently also have geographical spheres.

Angels are actually seen to assist one another in the spiritual warfare taking place, probably at this very moment.

35. One angel is named twice in this chapter. Who is it (Daniel 10:13)?

    M_____.

DALE AND CATHY HANCOCK

Michael is one of only two angels named in the Bible. He is referred to as the "archangel" (Jude 9). The other is Gabriel, the messenger angel to Zechariah regarding John's birth and to Mary regarding Jesus's birth.

36. Read Daniel 10:21. What is Michael referred to as?

Y_____ prince.

Michael is Daniel's prince, the prince of his people, Israel. We will see more on this protective relationship with Israel in chapter 12.

Read Daniel 11. Once again Daniel is given incredibly detailed information on the northern (Seleucid) and southern (Ptolemy or Egyptian) kingdoms, the two strongest kingdoms to emerge from the Grecian conquest under Alexander. The events wouldn't happen for several hundred years. The information is so specific and detailed that some liberal scholars think it had to have been written after the fact. It is sad to think there are students of the Word that actually discount God's sovereign omniscience. The specificity is actually tremendously important. Every detail of this happened during the intertestamental period as recorded in history, just as the angel said it would. We can trust the specificity of all end-time information.

Much explanation is given regarding the conflict between the northern and southern kingdoms, with Israel geographically grappling between them. By Daniel 11:21–35, however, the narrative entails the activities and character of Antiochus Epiphanies. It is like reading a history book before events happens.

Then there is a shift in the narrative by 11:40 or perhaps as early as 11:36. We previously learned that Antiochus Epiphanies was a type of the Antichrist to come, but now we skip to the "time of the end" (11:40), with detailed descriptions of the activities and character of the Antichrist. And though tens of thousands shall fall, two specific countries are delivered out of his hand.

37. What countries are delivered from the hand of the Antichrist (11:41)?

E_____ and M_____ and the main part of the A_____.

We know these lands today as modern-day southern Jordan.

It is intriguing that Daniel is told that these specific lands are unavailable to the Antichrist. Jesus's instructions are to flee (Matthew 24:16; Mark 13:14; and Luke 21:21) when the Antichrist will reveal himself in the temple as the abomination that makes the temple desolate. We know from Revelation 12 that the woman (the remnant of Jews who wouldn't bow to Antichrist) escapes the pursuit of Satan and is protected for the second half of the seventieth week or 1,260 days. Many Bible teachers say those who flee are protected in the ancient city of Petra, located in southern Jordan, ancient Edom and Moab, the lands that are delivered from the Antichrist's hand. Wandering through that ancient place with hundreds of caves in the pink stone, we were easily able to imagine the woman of Revelation 12 being protected there.

Read Daniel 12. Chapter 12 opens with, "At that time," referring to the previous verses that dealt with Antichrist's activities during the time of the end. At that time, the time of the end, a unique event occurs in heaven. Michael, Israel's protector, who has charge of them, shall rise or stand (12:1).

38. What ensues when Michael rises (12:1)?

> "T_____ such has n_____ been" since the nation of Israel began.

Throughout history, Israel has experienced much trouble, but at this time, the time of the end, it is worse than ever before or ever will be.

Jesus refers to this time as the great tribulation (Matthew 24:21; Mark 13:19).

Now, what does Michael have to do with this? Many scholars believe Michael stands or rises to protect, and that may well be the case. However, the Hebrew word for "stand" is *amad*; it means to stand, to stand up, or to stand still.[23] Michael *has* been protecting Israel probably since her birth. But at this point, at the height of her trouble, it may be that he stands still.

39. For more insight into this, read 2 Thessalonians 2:1–9 and fill in the blanks.

> The restrainer must be taken "o_____ of the w_____" (2 Thessalonians 2:7). And then the lawless one (Antichrist) will be "r_____" (2:6).
>
> At the point the restrainer is removed, the man of lawlessness will take (2 Thessalonians 2:4) "…his seat in the t_____ of God, proclaiming
> h_____ to be God [in the middle of the seventieth week].

The identity of the restrainer has long been a mystery. Some who place the timing of the rapture before the seventieth week believe the restrainer to be the Holy Spirit—that He is evacuated from earth with the church at the rapture. But the Holy Spirit is God, and He doesn't require us to be present for His habitation.

There are some who believe the restrainer to be human government, with laws and consequences keeping the chaos under control. But human government hasn't been entirely successful at just keeping mild vicissitudes at bay, much less the man or the devil.

---

[23] Zodhiates, *Hebrew-Greek Key,* 1991.

The restrainer has been holding back the revelation of the Antichrist until he, the restrainer, is taken out of the way. The restrainer may well be the protective archangel Michael, who has been holding him at bay and will someday stand still and allow the necessary events of the close of this age to unfold.

Now that puzzling war in heaven (Revelation 12:7–17) makes sense. Michael and his angels fight with Satan and his angels in the middle of the seventieth week. Michael wins and throws Satan to earth. We can almost see him brushing his hands clean of him in satisfaction. Satan can no longer at that point stand before the throne and accuse the brethren. He becomes infuriated because he knows his time is short, three and a half years. He comes after those who love Jesus when he cannot get to the Jewish remnant. Michael *amads*, stands still, and the events of the great tribulation are allowed to begin.

40. Read Daniel 12:2 and fill in the blanks. The angel briefly mentions *two* resurrections:

Some to e_____ life and some to shame and e_____ c_____.

Let's seek scripture to comment on this rather surprising and puzzling scripture. Jesus also spoke of the two resurrections.

41. Read John 5:28–29 and fill in the blanks.

Do not marvel at this … a_____ who are in the tombs will hear his voice and come out … (some to) … the resurrection of l_____ and (some) to the resurrection of j_____.

It would seem that Revelation 20:11–15 is also speaking of this and makes it clear that our eternity is based in Christ, His finished work on the cross, and His having written our name in the book of life (Revelation 20:15). Our salvation is the *free* gift of God. Though chilling to realize, as Daniel is told and as Jesus said, *all* will be resurrected, just at different times and for two vastly different destinations.

In Daniel 12:7, the three and a half years—a time, times, and half a time—are again noted, and Daniel is told not once but twice to shut and seal the words of the scroll (book) he has written, because the words are for the time of the end (12:4, 9). These words—these powerful, prophetically specific, and sometimes confusing (even for Daniel) words—are protected and kept for the generation at the end of the age, who will so desperately need them. Daniel pleads to know the outcome, but he is reassured again to go his way, that he shall rest (die) and stand in his allotted place (be resurrected) at the end of the days (12:13).

42. Finally, in verses 12:11–12, we see some heretofore never-mentioned numbers of days—1,290 and 1,335. (You may want to skip this portion of the workbook because we

cannot be dogmatic about the meaning of these numbers. But if you want some extra credit, let's do some calendar math.)

Up to this point, all time segments have been equal to three and a half years (forty-two months, 1,260 days, a time, times, and half a time). Now we see 1,290 and 1,335.

1,290 days represent an added _____ days to the usual 1,260 days.
1,335 days represent an added _____ days to the usual 1,260 days.

Our best understanding of the additional thirty days is that this is the time needed for the bowl judgments of Revelation. The conditions brought about by the events associated with the bowls may well be incompatible with life—living under a scorching sun with no drinkable water; thirty days are probably the extent to which life could endure.

43. As to the additional seventy-five days, check your phone or insurance company calendar with the Jewish holidays and count the days (beginning at sundown) from Yom Kippur to Hanukkah. How many days? _____

There are seventy-five days between these festivals and always have been. Yom Kippur is Israel's Day of Atonement. Year after year, before the temple was destroyed, this was the only day when the high priest could go into the holy of holies to make atonement for the sin of the people and himself.

Hanukkah, though not one of the seven Levitical feasts, was the celebration of the rededication of the temple after Antiochus Epiphanes desolated it.

Someday after Jesus returns in glory, the remnant, those Jews who didn't submit to Antichrist, will look on "Him whom they have pierced and … mourn … as one mourns for an only child" (Zechariah 12:10); and they will see that all along Jesus was their Messiah. Those who place their faith in Jesus, Yeshua, will experience their real Day of Atonement. He will pour out His grace at their pleas for mercy and be their ultimate atonement, their salvation, because salvation has *always* been in Christ alone.

The additional seventy-five days *may* be to allow for the cleansing (like Hanukkah) accomplished by the bowls and the rebuilding and rededication of an earthly temple, where He will tabernacle among His people during the millennium (Ezekiel 40–48; Revelation 20).

Much of this is speculation, and we can just be like Daniel, go our way, rest in Him, and trust Him. These things won't be understandable until the days of the end. But rest assured in your bewilderment—He has this all figured out, to the day.

THE MINOR PROPHETS

The last twelve books of the Old Testament are often called the "Minor Prophets" because in general they are shorter than the five books of the Major Prophets.

For the purpose of this study, we will focus on only those portions *directly* related to eschatological (end-time) information.

CHAPTER 22

HOSEA

The book of Hosea is beautiful but harsh, using the metaphor of a faithful husband with a terribly unfaithful wife to demonstrate God's redeeming love for His people in light of their great sinfulness. It was written to the northern ten tribes before their Assyrian captivity.

Though very little directly entails the latter days, we see the already-but-not-yet paradigm.

Read Hosea 11:10–11.

> The Lord will "r_____ like a l_____ and His children will come t_____ from the west ... from Egypt ... and ... Assyria ... and return to their h_____."

He did, and He will. They did, and they are.

CHAPTER 23

JOEL

The theme of the book of Joel is the day of the Lord, the judgment of God on the nations and Israel. The day of the Lord's wrath is exemplified in a terrible, devastating locust invasion. Once again, it happened "already but not yet." Historical events are used to foreshadow and prepare us for what is to come.

God's wrath over the sinfulness of man is demonstrated, but as we repeatedly see, His grace and mercy are available for the repentant, for those who call on the name of the Lord. For them, that day isn't a day of His wrath but one of restoration and protection.

There is much to learn about the great and terrible day of the Lord in Joel.

1. Read Joel 2:1–2 and circle all that apply. The day of the Lord is

    a. a day of alarm and trembling;
    b. a day like never before or since;
    c. a bright, sunshiny day; or
    d. a day of thick darkness and gloom.

2. What musical instrument is associated with it?

    T_____.

Recall that Jesus and Paul spoke of trumpets sounding when the Lord returns.

3. Read Joel 2:10–11. What cosmic calamities are associated with it?

    Heavens t_____.
    Sun and moon are d_____.
    Stars withdraw their s_____.

4. Read Acts 2:16–21 along with Joel 2:28–32. Use both of these passages to fill in the blanks.

When Peter preached his first sermon at Pentecost, he quoted the prophet Joel. In the last days, on whom shall the Spirit be poured?

A_____ flesh.
Young men shall see v_____.
Old men shall dream d_____.

In the last days, there will be profound manifestations of the Holy Spirit. When in Jerusalem recently, we heard of many Muslims and Jews who had dreams and visions of the Lord Jesus.

5. At what point will the cosmic calamities, the sun darkening and moon turning to blood, occur (Joel 2:31; Acts 2:20)?

   a. Before the great and awesome day of the Lord comes
   b. When the great and awesome day of the Lord comes
   c. After the great and awesome day of the Lord comes

These frightening events occur before the day of God's wrath to herald that it is coming.

6. Who then shall be saved?

   E_____ who calls upon the name of the L_____.

7. This all sounds very familiar, doesn't it? Review Matthew 24:29–30, along with Mark 13:24–26, for the sequence of these events.

When do the cosmic events occur? Circle all that apply.

   b. Immediately after the great tribulation
   c. Before Jesus comes in the clouds to gather His elect
   d. After Jesus comes in the clouds to gather His elect

The heralding signs in the heavens will occur immediately after the great tribulation and just before the Lord Jesus returns in the clouds. When He returns, He will rescue His own and begin His day, the day of the Lord.

Luke 21:28 tells us to raise our heads, to look up in expectation when we see these signs come upon the earth, for redemption, our deliverer, is coming.

Yet even at this point, as God declares through Joel, there is a chance for true repentance.

8. Read Joel 2:12–13 and fill in the blanks.

    For the Lord, your God, "is g_____ and m_____."

9. Read Acts 2:21 and fill in the blanks.

    And … e_____ who call upon the name of the Lord shall be s_____.

Our Lord is abounding in steadfast love, and even in the chaos of these events, even then, one may call on Him and be saved.

And someday, after His wrath has been poured out, there will be a glorious future for Jerusalem.

10. Read Joel 3:16–21. What will Jerusalem be (3:17)?

    H_____.

11. How long shall Judah be inhabited (3:20)?

    F_____.

As He has promised through His Word, there is a glorious future for Jerusalem.

Answer Key: 1. a, b, d
                  5. a
                  7. b, c

CHAPTER 24

AMOS

The book of Amos was written during a time of wealth and prosperity in Israel, a very dangerous time for God's people. In their self-absorption, the nation of Israel expected God's wrath to fall on their enemies, not on them. Amos warned them that judgment was also going to fall on them.

1. Read Amos 5:18–24; 6:1–8. What is promised for those who long for the day of the Lord to come on others (5:18)?

    W_____.

What is promised for those at ease in Zion (6:1)?

    W_____.

What is promised for those who lie on beds of ivory, sing idle songs, drink wine from bowls, and are not grieved (over sin) (6:4–7)?

    W_____.

Oh, how easy it is to be lulled into complacency when we are comfortable and without a sense of need. But knowing that the day of the Lord *is* coming should spur us on to share the good news of salvation through Christ.

Finally, in the last verses of Amos, we find promises of ultimate restoration, a golden age for Israel.

2. Read 9:11–15. What does God declare (9:15)?

    I will plant them on their l_____, and they shall never again be uprooted out of the l_____ I have given them.

We, the church, cannot ignore the importance of the actual land of Israel to our God.

CHAPTER 25

OBADIAH

In the very brief book of Obadiah, we see that, though God uses Israel's enemies to discipline her, those enemies are still accountable to Him and will experience the day of the Lord.

Read Obadiah 15 and fill in the blanks.

> For the day of the Lord is near upon all the n_____. As you have done it, it s_____ be d_____ to y_____; your deeds shall r_____ on your own head.

There is a divine recompense for the mistreatment of Israel. This *may* be what is in view in the sheep and goat judgment of Matthew 25, but it is difficult to say.

CHAPTER 26

JONAH

Try as we might, there just isn't anything directly related to end-time events in the humorous, wonderful, true, and fantastic book of Jonah. But we can't miss the steadfast love of our merciful God, the God of second and seventy-times-seven chances.

CHAPTER 27

MICAH

As with the other prophets, the themes of judgment and restoration sing back and forth with the promise of ultimate peace and prosperity forever.

Because of her transgressions, Jerusalem "shall become a heap of ruins," but God has promised some glorious things in the latter days, even a change in the geography of Jerusalem.

1. Read Micah 4:1–7. What will happen to the mountain of the house of God (4:1)?

    It "shall be established as the h_____ of mountains."

We also saw this prophecy of the dramatic change in the topography of Jerusalem in Isaiah 2.

2. What will the nations say?

    Come, let us go u__ to the mountain of the Lord … that He may t_____
    us His ways and that we may w_____ in His paths.

3. How long will the Lord reign over them in Mount Zion (Jerusalem)?

    F_____.

4. Read Micah 5:1–5. Jesus is prophesied to be born in Bethlehem but also to shepherd His flock in majesty.

How will his flock dwell (5:4–5)?

    S_____.

5. Why are they secure?

    Because their shepherd is "g_____ to the ends of the earth. And he shall
    be their p_____."

These prophecies have been fulfilled already in Christ but not yet to the glorious degree they
shall be.

CHAPTER 28

NAHUM

Like Jonah, Nahum doesn't reveal any specific end-times information. It's a sad sequel to the book of Jonah. Nineveh repented and turned from their wicked ways in response to Jonah's short sermon. By the time of Nahum, however (set many years later), their demise was certain. The Lord restored the majesty of Jacob as the majesty of Israel (Nahum 2:2).

CHAPTER 29

HABAKKUK

In Habakkuk we read the reassuring promise of the ultimate conclusion of the age. While our world becomes increasingly chaotic as we advance toward the future latter days, these reassuring verses will need to be engraved on our hearts.

1. Read Habakkuk 2:14 and fill in the blanks.

   For the earth w_____ b_____ filled with the k_____ of the glory of the Lord.

2. Read Habakkuk 2:20 and fill in the blanks.

   But the Lord is in His holy t_____; let all the e_____ keep s_____ before Him.

A day is coming when reverence for, and knowledge of, the Lord *will* fill the earth. As our world grows more and more irreverent without regard for the truth of His Word, how does this blessed assurance of His future reign make you feel?

CHAPTER 30

ZEPHANIAH

Zephaniah focuses more on the subject of the day of the Lord than any other prophet. The two-fold aspect of that day, judgment followed by blessing, is presented repeatedly with near and distant-future fulfillment in view. Zephaniah prophesied during the days of good King Josiah with warnings to repent and prophecies of the ultimate restoration for the faithful remnant of his people.

1. Read Zephaniah 1:14–18. Here we learn more about the characteristics of the day of the Lord in no uncertain terms.

What words are used to describe that *day* (1:14–15)?

It is n_____.
It is b_____.
The m_____ man c_____ aloud.
It is a day of w_____.
It is a day of d_____.
It is a day of a_____.
It is a day of r_____.
It is a day of d_____.
It is a day of d_____.
It is a day of g_____.

2. What musical instrument is associated with that day (1:16)?

T_____ blast.

Again, we see trumpets involved in the last days. Throughout the Old Testament, we see God using trumpets to call His people to himself (recall Mt. Sinai) and to go to war. That is exactly what He will do at the day of the Lord.

3. What element is associated with that day (1:18)?

    F_____.

4. What shall it consume (1:18)?

    S_____ the earth … for a f_____ and s_____ end he will make
    of all the i_____ of the earth.

Recall 2 Peter 3:7–10. This earth and heavens are reserved for fire, and yet the Lord continues to urge them to repentance before that day comes.

5. Read Zephaniah 2:1–3. Whom do we seek to be hidden from the Lord's anger?

    The L_____.

Only the Lord is our refuge from the wrath of the Lord. And there is always the promise of restoration for the faithful remnant.

6. Read Zephaniah 2:9; 3:9–20. What type of people will be left in Israel who will seek refuge in the Lord (3:12)?

    H_____ and l_____.

7. What lands will the remnant of His people, the survivors of His nation, plunder and possess (2:9)?

    M_____ and A_____.

Now it may be a stretch, but recall in Daniel 11:41 that these lands, Moab and Amnon, along with Edom, were delivered *out* of the hand of the Antichrist. Though the Word of God gives us very little information regarding the location, we know from Matthew 24:16 and Mark 13:14 that God tells those in Jerusalem to flee to the mountains when they see the abomination of desolation.

For greater clarity and information regarding this, read Revelation 12:6, 14–16. The woman (Israel) flees to the wilderness to a place of God's protection, where Satan is unable to reach her. Look at a Bible map of ancient and modern-day lands. Edom, Moab, and Ammon were in present-day Jordan, where the ancient city of Petra lies. It is nestled among the mountains and largely attainable only through the narrow Siq, a dim, high-walled gorge that winds through the pink rock of the ancient Nabatean city. When we walked down to the iconic Treasury, made famous by Indiana Jones, the horse-drawn carriages that plummet along the narrow way almost ran us over. Many Bible teachers speculate that Petra could be the location of protection for those who flee when the Antichrist is revealed.

8. Finally, read Zephaniah 3:17. At last, when their fortunes are restored and His people are renowned among the peoples of the earth, the Lord God will be in the midst of His people.

What will He do (3:17)?

He will r_____ … with g_____.
He will q_____ you by His l_____.
He will e_____ … with l_____ s_____.

Have you ever thought of God singing over you? He will. Loudly!

CHAPTER 31

HAGGAI

Haggai was written after the return of the exiles from Babylon. It was written to the leaders of Jerusalem to motivate them to finish rebuilding the temple. As such, there is no explicit end-time material, but God promised to fill the house with His glory, a glory greater than that seen in the former temple.

This could possibly be a reference to Christ's first coming when He was physically present in the temple. Recall that the glory of God, the Shekinah, had departed in Ezekiel's day. When Christ came, His glory was present, though veiled, and unrecognized by most.

At His Second Coming, He will be unveiled, and His glory will fill not only the temple but also the whole earth.

CHAPTER 32

ZECHARIAH

Zechariah was written to returning Babylonian exiles and is a most difficult book to understand. It is highly symbolic, more so than even Revelation.

We will strive to point out verses that are directly eschatological and cross-reference when possible. There are many passages from Zechariah referred to or alluded to in the New Testament, mostly in Revelation.

1. Read Zechariah 2:6–13 and fill in the blanks. What is God's heart toward Israel, particularly Jerusalem, as He plans to come and dwell in their midst (2:8)?

    She is "the a_____ of His e_____."

2. What city will He again choose (2:12)?

    J_____.

3. Read Zechariah 3:1–2. This is one of two instances (see also Job 1:6–12; 2:1–7) in the Old Testament narrative, in which Satan appears to have some kind of access to the throne room and the presence of the Lord.

What is he doing to the high priest, Joshua (3:1)?

    A_____ him.

As we will see in Revelation 12:10, that ancient foe has been accusing the brethren day and night. Someday the Lord will put an end to that.

Zechariah 8 is a beautiful foretelling of the peace and prosperity promised to the faithful remnant. He also assures them of real estate, with the elderly sitting in the streets and boys and girls playing (8:4–5). He assures them that His people will come from the east and the west to dwell in Jerusalem (8:7). He assures them there will be peace and produce, and that Judah and Israel will be a blessing (8:12–13).

4. Read the entire chapter of Zechariah 8. Where will many people and strong nations go to seek the Lord of hosts (8:22)?

    J_____.

What will people from nations of every tongue do (8:23)?

    They will take hold of the robe of a J_____ saying, "Let u_____ go w_____ you for we have heard that G_____ is with you."

5. Read 9:9–10 to see a prophecy of both Christ's first and second comings. How did Jesus come the first time (9:9)?

    Jerusalem … your king is coming to you … h_____ and mounted on a d_____, on a c_____, the foal of a donkey.

As we know, that is exactly what happened at His first coming. On the Sunday before His death, burial, and resurrection, Palm Sunday, He rode into Jerusalem on a donkey. At His Second Coming, He won't be humbly riding on a donkey.

What will be the extent of His rule at His Second Coming (9:10)?

    From sea to sea … to the e_____ of the e_____.

Like Isaiah 9:6–7, this reign hasn't been fulfilled literally as yet, but it will be.

And now we come to the *really* difficult portion of Zechariah. Chapters 12–14 are perhaps the most profoundly eschatological and apocalyptic literature in all scripture. The day of the

6. Read Zechariah 12–14. Now read them again. (Trust us.)

Our best understanding of these passages is that we are reading of the events that will take place *during* the day of the Lord, specifically what the Jews in Jerusalem will experience after the Lord's return. Before the day of the Lord, the nations will have gathered against Jerusalem, and the Antichrist will have his headquarters there. Apparently, thankfully, some will repent and recognize their Messiah.

7. Read 13:8–9. What fraction of the people will say, "The Lord is my God"? (Not you, Antichrist!)

    ___ /___

It may be this third of the house of David who will realize that Yeshua, Jesus, was always their Messiah.

8. Read Zechariah 12:10–11. What will they do when they see Him (12:10)?

    When they look on me, on Him whom they have p_____, they shall
    m_____ for Him as one mourns for an o_____ c_____, and
    w_____ bitterly over him, as one weeps over a firstborn.

With great sorrow and repentance, some of Israel's inhabitants will experience God's grace and mercy when they look on the returning King and see His hands and feet. They will see that He was pierced. The mourning and remorse will be profound when they realize He is and was Messiah all along. Yet note it is individuals who are mourning (12:12); families and wives will be by themselves, because salvation has always been, and always will be given, by grace through faith in Christ alone.

This event may well be the fulfilling completion of the feast, Yom Kippur, Israel's Day of Atonement.

9. Read Zechariah 13:1. What will happen on this day of repentance and mourning?

    On that day there shall be a f_____ opened for the house of D_____
    and the inhabitants of J_____, to c_____ them from their
    s_____ and uncleanness.

They will see Jesus, Yeshua, their Messiah; mourn over their sins; repent; be cleansed and forgiven of their sins; and be His forevermore.

In chapter 14, we continue to see the battle of the nations against Jerusalem. Recall Luke 21:20–24, in which Jerusalem is surrounded by armies.

10. Read Zechariah 14:1–5. Who is it that is fighting against the nations (14:3)?

    The L_____.

As He stood on the Mount of Olives, just as the angels assured His disciples He would do at His Second Coming (Acts 1:11), an incredible event occurred.

11. Draw what you are reading in verses 14:4–5.

North

West   East

South

This earthquake may correspond with the seventh and last bowl of Revelation 16:17–19 (and recall Ezekiel 38–39). The topography is forever changed, and Jerusalem remains aloft to forever dwell in s_____ (Zechariah 14:11). Recall Isaiah 2:2 and Micah 4:1.

It seems that the book could end there with a nice "happily ever after," but wait. God isn't finished with those who waged war on Jerusalem.

12. Read 14:12–13. What happens to their flesh, eyes, and tongues?

They r_____ while they are still standing on their feet.

Though this sounds like a nuclear event, we will soon see the horrific effects of the bowls when we study Revelation 16. This is most likely a result of the bowl judgments, the conclusion of the wrath of God.

13. Finally, read 14:16–21. What feast or festival is mentioned repeatedly?

The Feast of B_____ or Tabernacles.

The joyous seventh and final feast of the Jewish Levitical calendar is completed. All the spring feasts were completed at His first coming. With the Second Coming, the fall feasts will be enacted and completed, fulfilled. Our Lord Jesus will for all time tabernacle or dwell among His people in peace and security.

CHAPTER 33

MALACHI

We now come to the last of the writing prophets, the last book of the Old Testament. Malachi wrote as a wake-up call to urge Israel to renewed covenant fidelity. Giving and tithing had diminished (always a bad sign), people were bringing less than their best to God, and marriages were marked by faithlessness. Though the book was written over twenty-four hundred years ago, how relevant it is today.

1. Read Malachi 2:14–15. What did God make husband and wife to be?

   O_____.

What is God seeking?

   G_____ o_____.

Who knows? It may be to our very offspring that the Lord returns. We must be diligent in passing on our faith and knowledge.

2. Read Malachi 3–4. These verses have much to do with the day of the Lord. Here we learn that an old prophet will have a role to play in the return of Christ. There is to be a messenger who will prepare the way of the Lord.

Who is he (3:1; 4:5)?

   E_____.

When does he come?

   B_____ me [the Lord]. (3:1)
   B_____ the great and awesome day of the Lord comes. (4:5)

When the Lord returns, the day of the Lord begins. Elijah must come before that day, before the Lord's return.

During His first coming, Jesus's disciples asked Him about Elijah's coming.

3. Read Matthew 17:10–13. Jesus clearly explained to them that Elijah would come and that he had *already* come.

Who had he come as?

J_____ the B_____.

John was not a reincarnation. That is a non-biblical belief. John was a *type* of Elijah, fulfilling that roll. In fact, in Luke 7:27, Jesus quoted the Malachi 3:1 passage regarding John.

Just as John came preaching repentance at Christ's first coming, we know Elijah will come again just before the day of the Lord, just as Jesus said he would.

4. For additional information on this, read Revelation 11:3–14. The vast majority of scholars agree that one of these two witnesses who testify for the last half of the seventieth week, the 1,260 days, is Elijah. The other is probably Moses. This is based on the unusual circumstances surrounding their deaths, their representation of the Law and the Prophets, the powers they have during the 1,260 days, as well as their presence at the transfiguration.

If that is the case, Elijah is seen here as physically present *before* the day of the Lord, just as Malachi 4:5 said he would be. Elijah and Moses will be testifying throughout the second half of the seventieth week—through the great tribulation and then the day of the Lord.

Because of these passages in Malachi, to this day observant Jews are still waiting for Elijah to come and herald the Messiah's *first* coming. As part of the beloved Passover Seder, a chair is left empty for him, a beautiful cup is reserved for him, and a child is sent to the door to see whether he is there—all parts of a time-honored tradition.[24] As believers, we know Elijah already came and that Messiah already came—and that yes, they will come again.

The day of the Lord is coming. Nothing should serve to spur us on to enjoy the privilege of sharing the gospel more than this knowledge. As 2 Peter 3:9–10 reminds us, the Lord is patient, not wishing anyone to perish, but the day of the Lord will come.

5. Read Malachi 4:1–3 and fill in the blanks.

For the evildoers, "the day that is coming shall s_____ them a_____."

---

[24] Howard and Rosenthal, *Feasts of the Lord*, 59

Recall that Peter told us that the heavens and earth that now exist are stored up for fire.

6. But for those who fear His name, what will that day bring (Malachi 4:2)?

    H_____ in its w_____ … leaping like c_____ from the s_____.

What a happy picture! Once again, we see that, based on our position in Christ, His return and His day will bring either judgment or rescue and blessing.

So, brothers and sisters, we finish part 2 of this study. Next, we move into Revelation to complete our picture and wrap up all the layers of information you have mined.

But so far, you know much. Fill in the chart below. It will serve to help you keep the information orderly and easily recalled. The seventieth week is divided with a midpoint. Down the side is a column of the various groups affected in profoundly different ways. Recall as much as you can. Draw connecting lines to the sequence line for time reference and record how the events affect the different groups. You know more than you think.

_____•_____

Believers/The church
Nonbelievers
Jews
Believing Jews (Messianic)
Antichrist
Satan
Elijah
Michael
Jesus
Those in Jerusalem

PART 3

THE REVELATION

Introduction

The book of Revelation is the unveiling of the majesty and ultimate, eternal glory of our Lord and Savior Jesus Christ. In it we see Him as He is, the King of kings, and Lord of lords. We should approach the content just as John did, by falling on our faces before Him.

It's easy to agonize over what the content *means* (usually in the limited light of our own experience) to the point that we miss what it simply *says*. Therefore, we have attempted to rightly divide the Word into bite-sized pieces so we can be blessed by what it says. Revelation is the only book of the Bible that comes with a promise of blessing for simply reading it or hearing it read.

It is a visual book. John is told to write what he sees. We will see John's vision by drawing it. Don't worry if you have no artistic ability. Stick figures work nicely. Sketching will help us to visualize the action and the players in the scenes. It is a very dynamic book, full of fascinating characters and a great deal of activity. Most of what you draw will be symbolic; the book is highly symbolic throughout. But that doesn't negate its reality; the symbols serve to deepen the description of never-before-seen things, characters, and events.

Your pictures will be fun to share because this study is best done with a group. Many of the questions are intended to be discussed with others, so the material becomes more personal to you. Let us begin.

Amen, come, Lord Jesus!

CHAPTER 34

AN INTRODUCTION AND A VISION. REVELATION 1

1. Read Revelation 1:1–4. What or who does this book reveal?

    a. The future
    b. Prophecy
    c. End-time events
    d. Jesus Christ

It's important to keep in mind that the book is *the* revelation (singular) of Jesus Christ, *not revelations* of end-time events. The book is about Him and His glory, not about us and our curiosity about the future.

2. God gave the revelation of Jesus to Jesus to show His servants (us) some things. What things?

    Things that must s_____ take place.

The Greek word for "soon" is *tachos.*[25] It means many episodes occurring within a brief space of time quickly or speedily. Someday the future events that will unveil the full majesty and glory of Jesus Christ will begin to unfold rapidly (soon) within a brief span of time under God's divine plan. These *things* will bring this present age to a close. In Revelation, we are privy to the unfolding of a future conflict. It is one Jesus has already won, but it has yet to be enacted on the stage of human history.

---

[25] *New Strong's Exhaustive Concordance.*, 89 of the Greek dictionary portion

3. But who is blessed by the words of this prophecy?

The one who r_____ a_____ the words.
Those who h_____, and who k_____ [guard or take to heart] what is written in it.

4. Why do you think hearing and keeping the content of Revelation will be a blessing to you?

_____

_____

_____

5. Read Revelation 1:4–6 and fill in the blanks. To whom is the book dedicated (1:5–6)?

To him who l_____ us and has f_____ us from our sins by his blood and made us a kingdom, p_____ to his God and F_____.

Revelation is not only about Jesus and from Jesus; it is dedicated to Jesus. His blood released us from the bondage of sin, and He made us priests, privileged to be in His Father's holy presence. What an incredible position He has placed us in—already.

6. Read Revelation 1:7 and fill in the blanks below.

After a benediction of praise at the end of verse 6, it seems that John excitedly recorded the rest of the story, the manner of Christ's return, and the reaction of the world. Recall that John had watched the ascension of Jesus as He was "lifted up and a cloud took him out of their sight" (Acts 1:9). The angels told John and the other disciples that Jesus would come back the same way they had seen Him go into heaven, in the clouds.

Who will see Him when He comes in the clouds?

E_____ eye … even those who p_____ him.

Everyone on earth will witness the return of Christ.

Who do you think are those who pierced him? Consider and discuss.

_____

Recall that he was pierced for our transgressions.

What will be the response of all the tribes of the earth?

They will w_____ on account of him.

As we saw in parts 1 and 2 of our study, we again notice the dichotomous response of the world to the return of Jesus. Recall Matthew 24:30. "Then will appear in heaven the sign of the Son of Man, and then all the tribes of the earth will mourn, and they will see the Son of Man coming on the clouds of heaven with power and great glory."

Not everyone will be overjoyed to see our Lord return.

Who will wail and mourn?

_____.

Who will praise and rejoice?

_____.

7. Read Revelation 1:8–11. John is told to write what he *sees* in a book. He describes himself as a brother and partner with those to whom he writes. In what three things does he partner with them (1:9)?

The t_____, the k_____ and the p_____ e_____ that are in Jesus.

The original recipients of the letter probably knew John personally, or they certainly knew of him. Knowing he was experiencing tribulation along with them, needing patient endurance from Jesus, and looking forward to their joint membership in the kingdom were probably very comforting to them.

On the island called P_____ on account of the w_____ of God and the testimony of J_____.

Patmos is an island in the Aegean Sea, and there Rome exiled political prisoners. Early church tradition holds that John may have had some freedom of movement there, perhaps living in a little cave. He would have been very old, since the book was most likely written in the mid-90s during the reign of Emperor Domitian.[26]

---

[26] *The ESV Study Bible, notes, 2464*

To make this even more personal and meaningful, recall everything you know about the beloved apostle John and list it below.

John's bio:

We have compiled a list for you, but you probably thought of more.

- He was an apostle, one of the Twelve, one of the first Jesus called, along with his brother James and their fishing partners, Peter and Andrew.
- He was likely the only apostle alive by the time of this writing. According to church tradition, all the others had been martyred, his brother James being one of the first.
- He was present along with his brother and Peter at the transfiguration, the first unveiling of Jesus's glory.
- He felt particularly close to Jesus, sitting by His side at the Last Supper (which may have indicated that he was the youngest disciple), and he was referred to as the "beloved" (but only in his own Gospel). Perhaps we should all feel that way.
- He attended to Jesus in the garden of Gethsemane (though he fell asleep), and he was apparently the only disciple at the cross.
- Jesus charged him with the care of his mother; and according to church tradition, she indeed lived with him until she died.
- He was the first disciple to the empty tomb, though he let Peter enter first, and he was there to see Jesus ascend into heaven.
- He was an elder of the church of Ephesus and wrote the Gospel of John; 1, 2, and 3 John; and Revelation.

9. John was told to write what he saw in a book and send it to seven churches. What are the names of the churches (Revelation 1:11)?

_____, _____, _____,
_____, _____, _____.

We use the memory trick "ESP,TSP, & L" to help remember the names and their order. Look up the cities in your Bible map and sketch out the order of the destinations in a connect-the-dot format in the space below. Do you see it? The book was sent in an orderly fashion from point to point. It was actually the courier's route by which he would have carried a scroll from Patmos.[27] The book was to be circulated to those churches in those cities in that order.

10. Read Revelation 1:12–18. John turned to *see* the voice like a trumpet that told him to write what he saw and send it to those seven churches.

---

[27] *The ESV Study Bible*, notes, 2464.

Sketch what John saw.

Label your drawing and notice how often the word *like* is used, as though John is trying to compare the indescribable to something understood. You are making a sketch of our Lord, Jesus.

First Timothy 6:16 states that "God dwells in unapproachable light ... that no one has ever seen or can see Him." No wonder John's description is indescribable. Reread Daniel 7:9–10, 13–14 to further enhance your understanding and awe of His glory.

11. Now sketch John's response and Jesus's reassurance. Use speech bubbles.
    (Recall John's comfortable familiarity with Jesus at the Last Supper, how he leaned against Him; and notice his response now, when Christ is revealed in His full glory.)

How comforting to know that Jesus is the first and the last, the Alpha and the Omega, that He has the keys of death and Hades, and that He has this all under control. We have no need to fear.

12. Read Revelation 1:19–20. Jesus gave John the outline for the entire book. What is it?

Things that you h_____ seen,

those that are to t_____ p_____ after this.

The stage is set. The main character has been revealed. Now the outline is stated. In chapter 1, John wrote what he saw so far. In chapters 2–4, he will record the things that "are" and continue to be—the conditions of the church through the ages as well the current activity taking place in heaven. Then in chapters 5–22, he will record those things that *will* take place.

13. Finally, almost incidentally, Jesus explains the mystery of the seven stars and lampstands He is standing amid (1:20).

What are the seven stars? "A_____ of the seven c_____."

What are the seven lampstands? "The seven c_____."

Recall that we are the light of the world as believers. Pause here to pray that our own local churches will shine as an even brighter light for our communities and the world.

The word used for "angels" here could be heavenly, angelic messengers or even the human messengers, pastors. In chapters 2–3, Jesus addresses the encouragement and rebuke of each church to the angel, the representative of that particular church. We will see what Jesus has to say to these seven churches.

What do you think He would say to yours?

_____

_____

_____.

CHAPTER 35

JESUS'S LETTERS TO SEVEN CHURCHES. REVELATION 2 AND 3.

In these two chapters we find Jesus's letters to seven different churches. Scholars debate how to interpret and apply the information found in these letters, but the simplest position is to acknowledge that these churches were real, locatable churches of that day with actual issues pertinent to each one. The church throughout history has faced and continues to face the same issues.

We study the letters of Paul to seven different churches perhaps far more often than we study the brief, sometimes scathing, letters of Jesus to seven churches. The churches of the first century needed these words of Jesus. We need them even more today. As the end of this age approaches, the issues and conditions He addresses will likely worsen dramatically as the enemy fights the effectiveness of the church.

Each church is addressed in the same format, making the content easy to place in a chart for better understanding. First, Jesus describes Himself; then He usually has some positive words, (but not for Sardis or Laodicea), followed by some rebuke or negative comments (but not for Smyrna and Philadelphia). Finally, He gives the solution or encouragement, followed by the consequences for continued disobedience, and a promise for those who overcome—the conquerors.

1. Read chapters 2–3 and fill in the chart.

Church	Description	Positive	Negative	Solution	Consequences	Promise for Overcomers
Ephesus						
Smyrna						
Pergamum						
Thyatira						
Sardis						
Philadelphia						
Laodicea						

2. Now that you have closely examined the churches, draw lines to match the predominant characteristic with the appropriate church.

Ephesus	The Tolerant Church
Smyrna	The Compromising Church
Pergamum	The Dead Church
Thyatira	The Loveless Church
Sardis	The Persecuted Church
Philadelphia	The Materialistic Church
Laodicea	The Faithful Church

Though Ephesus was orthodox and correct in their doctrine, they were no longer as *loving* as they had been at first. They were admonished to "do the works they had done at first." Love is a verb.

Though the church in Smyrna was persecuted and poverty stricken because of the legalistic, religious Jews, they were encouraged, even in the face of martyrdom, to conquer. By doing so, they would be unharmed by the second death.

In Pergamum, where one of the first martyrs, Antipas, was burned for his faith, they had begun to compromise, to go along with the appearance of emperor worship to feed their families. Jesus assured them that He would be their provision with hidden manna and a special white stone, used in those days as a ticket to enter the victor's banquet.[28]

In Thyatira, their loving, serving attitude had become openly tolerant of immorality among them. Jesus encouraged those who hadn't succumbed to that tolerance to hold fast to the truth to the end.

Sardis receives the strongest rebuke, words that chill the very soul. They are a dead church. But disturbingly, they have a reputation of being alive. It is to this church that Jesus says He will come as a thief against them. But even in this church, there are those who belong to Him and those whose names He will never blot from His book.

Philadelphia is faithful and patiently enduring, though maligned by the religious. Jesus assures them of His protection and that their persecutors will *know* that He loves them.

Finally, Laodicea's materialism and pride so disgust Jesus that He longs to spew them from His mouth. Despite this, He loves this disgusting, lukewarm church; He is graciously knocking on the outside of their door, desiring their repentance and fellowship with Him.

---

[28] *The ESV Study Bible, notes, 2466*

It is encouraging to see that in each church, even in those with no positive remarks, there are still those He finds faithful and true. Oh, may we be found faithful and true in whatever community of believers we are part of.

3. Think about and discuss the following:

- How does Jesus's description of Himself specifically relate to each church in regard to its situation, strengths, and weaknesses?

    _____.

- What characteristic does He value and treasure in each church? What pleases Him in His church?

    _____.

- Discuss His reaction to sin in His church. Does He take it lightly?

    _____.

- Do you think any or all of these conditions and characteristics still exist in churches today?

    _____.

- What about your church?

    _____.

Before moving into chapter 4, the throne room of Heaven, it must be mentioned that many place the timing of the rapture at this point—because the word *church* isn't mentioned after chapters 2 and 3. (But it is. At the very end of the book, Jesus says in summary, "I, Jesus, have sent my angel to testify to you about these things for the churches" [Revelation 22:16].)

Also in Revelation 3:10, Jesus assures the church at Philadelphia that He will "keep you from the hour of trial that is coming on the whole world, to try those who dwell on the earth."

Many scholars and teachers cite these and other verses (1 Thessalonians 1:10; 5:9–10) as proof texts of God's evacuation of the church before trouble begins.

Surprisingly, rapture positions are somewhat a matter of semantics. The question is, is the tribulation the wrath of God? Or does the tribulation and greater, more intense tribulation (due to the Antichrist) *precede* the wrath of God?

We must be honest and consistent with God's Word. If Revelation 3:10 promises evacuation, what about Revelation 2:10? The church of Smyrna was faithful like Philadelphia, yet they were promised suffering and even admonished to continue being faithful unto death.

It's helpful to examine some of these words in the original Greek. In 3:10, the term "to keep" is *tereo* in the Greek, meaning "to watch over, guard, keep an eye on—not to keep out of or away from.[29] It is the same word used in Revelation 1:3 and 12:17 regarding keeping the words of the book of Revelation and keeping the commandments of God.

The word for "trial" in 3:10 is *peirazo* in the Greek, meaning "to test, prove, and even to tempt." It is the same word Jesus used in the Lord's Prayer regarding temptation.[30]

The Greek word for "tribulation" (not used in these verses) is *thlipsis,* meaning "pressure, anguish, persecution, burden, trouble."[31] Recall that in the Olivet Discourse, Jesus actually encouraged His believers that in the anguish of persecution, they would be used before the powerful and mighty, with the Holy Spirit giving them the words to speak. How believers respond to tribulation would thereby produce the greatest evangelical event in the history of the church, by which the gospel would finally be proclaimed throughout the world.

By allowing other scriptures to comment upon scripture, it appears that Jesus isn't telling the church of Philadelphia or any other believer that he or she is exempt from tribulation in this world. Believers are removed or rescued from the *wrath* of God (1 Thessalonians 5:9–10) but not from the pressure, anguish, persecution, and trouble of this world. Why would we think we are to be exempt from that, especially when we recall all the martyrs that have gone before us. He assures us that He is with us during whatever we go through—for His sake.

And now, with humble and awe-filled hearts, let us enter the throne room of heaven.

---

[29] Zodhiates, *Hebrew-Greek Key 1679.*
[30] Zodhiates, *Hebrew-Greek Key, 1661*
[31] Strong, *New Strong's Exhaustive Concordance,* 1632

CHAPTER 36

THE THRONE ROOM OF HEAVEN. REVELATION 4

If you still have your shoes on, you better kick them off. We are about to enter the throne room of heaven, holy ground indeed.

1. Read chapter 4 aloud. Who tells John to "come up here"? Refer to 1:10–14.

   a. Jesus
   b. Mighty Angel

(Note that at this point we have a "scene change." We will see this throughout the book of Revelation; sometimes action and events are taking place on earth and sometimes in heaven. As we read and study, always be aware of where we are.)

Jesus commands John to come up (to heaven). Again, there are many who equate this moment with the rapture of the church. Jesus tells John to come up so He can show him what must take place "after this," *this* being the conditions of the church as described in chapters 2–3. Again, this may well mean that after the church has experienced all her difficulties, the heavenly state and events described in the following chapters will transpire.

However, the Greek word for "after" is *meta,* meaning "amid, in the midst of, after, or among, implying accompaniment." It is the same word used of Jesus's coming *with* (*meta*) the clouds.[32] Therefore, Jesus's invitation to John may be to show him what is taking place in heaven *while* the church on earth is experiencing what had just been described in the seven letters.

2. As you listened to your reading of chapter 4, when do you think this glorious worship is taking place?

---

[32] Zodhiates, *Hebrew-Greek Key,* 1650

    a. In the distant past, before creation

    b. In the continuous present always: past, present, and future

    c. In the future after the church has been raptured and the millennium has begun

The answer is (b). This is what is going on in heaven right now and since before the dawn of time, and it will forever be. We know this because Old Testament prophets describe this same scene.

The conditions and problems facing the seven churches have been issues throughout the church age, and the worship scene we see in chapter 4 is continuous and eternal; therefore, it could be that Jesus is showing John what is and will be simultaneously taking place in heaven, not that the church has ceased to be on earth.

We are privy to the throne room of heaven in only a few passages of the Bible.

3. Read Isaiah 6:1–6 and note the similarities between the living creatures and the seraphim of Isaiah. How many wings do they have? _____

4. Read Ezekiel 1:4–28 and note the similarities of the living creatures as Ezekiel and John described them. What are their faces?

    M_____, O_____, L_____, E_____.

See Revelation 4:7 for the same description. We read here in Revelation what has taken place and will take place in heaven forever.

5. Is the One seated on the throne ever *specifically* described? _____

No, for no one has ever really seen God. He dwells, as 1 Timothy 6:16 says, in "unapproachable light." Rather than an actual detailed description, the words of John, Ezekiel, and Isaiah seem to give us more of their impressions. They all employ terms such as "likeness" and "appearance of" because He truly is indescribable. Even the use of jewels and gold conveys more the idea of power and profound value and glory instead of base stones and metals.

Write down some of your impressions of the throne room of heaven.

Phrases like "brilliantly bright" and "surrounding, penetrating praise" come to our mind. But really, like John and the prophets, it's hard to use mere words.

6. Now carefully reread chapter 4. Draw and label the throne room of heaven.

Like us, did you get cold chills just by drawing and picturing that and listening to the "rumblings and peals of thunder" amid the constant refrain of praise?

7. Besides "Him who sits on the throne," who are the other inhabitants of the throne room?

   Twenty-four e_____
   Four l _____ c_____

8. What do the four living creatures never stop saying (4:8)?

   H_____ _____ _____ __ ___ _____ ____ _____, _____
   ____ ____ __ ____ __ ___ c____.

9. And when the four living creatures say this, what do the twenty-four elders do (4:10)?

   F_____ down … w_____ him … (and) … c_____ their
   c_____ before the throne.

10. What do the twenty-four elders say (4:11)?

    W_____ are you, our L_____ and G_____, to receive g_____
    and h_____ and p_____, for you c_____ all things
    and by your w_____ they existed and were created.

Read the statements of the living creatures and the twenty-four elders aloud, like maybe every day. We will hear this glorious praise for eternity.

CHAPTER 37

THE SCROLL AND THE LAMB. REVELATION 5

In chapter 4, the veil was pulled back, and we were privileged to see and experience the glorious praise that will take place continuously in the throne room of heaven. Now, in chapter 5, we come to an event in heaven.

It is an event that, at the time of this writing, has probably not yet taken place. It is an event of such profundity that once it occurs, nothing will be the same on earth or in heaven. It is an event that will allow the subsequent unfolding of the rest of this age.

1. Read Revelation 5 aloud. In verse 1, John observes something in the hand of Him who is seated on the throne. What is it? Draw it.

2. In 5:2, John sees a strong angel. What question is he loudly proclaiming?

   Who is w_____ to o_____ the s_____ and
   b_____ its s_____?

3. What is John's response when no one in heaven or on earth or under the earth was able to open that scroll or look into it (5:4)?

   W_____ l_____.

The NIV version says, "He wept and wept." The Greek terms for his behavior are *klaio and polys*.[33] Taken together, they mean "to weep, wail, and mourn to the very greatest degree, to the uttermost—as one might weep who has no hope."[34]

---

[33] Zodhiates, *Hebrew-Greek Key, 2088*
[34] Zodhiates, *Hebrew-Greek Key, 4498*

We must pause and ask ourselves why.

4. Why is the beloved John weeping so inconsolably (5:4)?

    Because "n_____ one was found w_____."

What is so important about that scroll and its contents that John feels all is lost if it cannot be opened?

As we will see, without the opening of the scroll, we would continue forever in this present darkness. Oh, we can be redeemed and, when we die, be with Him in heaven; but there is so much more awaiting us. Someday we will be transformed, see Him as He is, and be *like* Him. Someday this earth and even heaven will be new. Someday Satan will be bound and finally thrown into the lake of fire.

But first that scroll in heaven has to be opened. The opening of that scroll is the beginning of the end. Without opening that scroll, we just go on as we are and have been forever. The events associated with the breaking of the seals, followed by the horrific conditions described within the scroll, serve to draw this age to its glorious finale. John wept because without the opening of that scroll, we can't arrive at the ultimate glorious point of the eternal perfect state.

Once the seals are opened, the scroll will unroll, and the day of the Lord, the foretold time of wrath, "the wrath of the Lamb," will commence on the earth.

5. What does one of the twenty-four elders essentially order John to do (5:5)?

    S_____ weeping.

6. Why does he tell him to stop weeping? Who can open the scroll?

    J_____!

7. By what two titles does the elder use to refer to Jesus (Revelation 5:5)?

    The L_____ of the tribe of J_____.
    (This is the only time in the Bible that He is referred to by that full title.)
    The R_____ of D_____.

8. Why can Jesus open the scroll? What qualifies Him to do so?

    He has c_____.

9. The text isn't explicit here as to what He has conquered, but from your Bible knowledge, what has He conquered to make Him worthy? List your thoughts below.

Do words like *sin*, *death*, *Satan*, and *hell* come to mind?

10. Though the elder referred to Him as the Lion, what did John see (5:6)?

    A L_____ *standing* as though it had been s_____. (emphasis added)

Jesus is our Lamb, the Lamb God provided for us, God's Lamb. He was upright on the cross. We aren't sure that is what is in view here, but we are sure that in heaven, the memory of the cross and His sacrificial death are forever precious.

11. Draw the scene John sees in Revelation 5:6–9. You may want to use comic-strip-style frames to show progression of action. Label each character and what he or she holds.

Read Daniel 7:9–10, 13–14. It may be that you just drew the dear old prophet's vision of this same scene centuries before Jesus came the first time. When God the Son took the scroll from God the Father, the stage was set for the beginning of the end of this age. It caused the living creatures and the twenty-four elders to be overcome with even more worship.

12. What do the golden bowls full of incense hold (5:8)?

    The p_____ of the s_____.

Perhaps these are the prayers of *all* saints throughout all the ages: "Thy Kingdom come."

God keeps our prayers, and like the incense of old, they are a sweet aroma to Him.

13. What is the adjective used to describe the song they sing?

    n_____.

They sing a new song before the Lamb that has never before been sung because that scroll has never before been opened.

14. Read Revelation 5:9–10 and sing this *new* song along with living creatures and elders.

15. How many angels join their voices with those of the living creatures and the elders (Revelation 5:11)?

    M_____ and m_____ and t_____
    and t_____.

16. Record their song below (5:12).

    _____

    _____

    _____

17. Who joins their voices now (5:13)?

    E_____ creature in h_____ and on e_____ and u_____
    the earth and in the s_____.

Record their song below.

_____

_____

Now read aloud all their songs that you have recorded … sing along!

Recall Philippians 2:6–11. The day is coming when *every* knee will bow.

CHAPTER 38

THE LAMB OPENS THE FIRST SIX SEALS. REVELATION 6

1. Read Revelation 6. After the glorious ceremony of chapter 5, the narrative continues in chapter 6 with Jesus opening the seals of that scroll. We see the first four seals associated with horses, popularly called the "four horses and riders of the apocalypse."

As Jesus opens the seals one by one, the living creatures take turns, commanding each horse to "come!"

The Greek word for "come," *erchomai*, means "to come, to go, to be going, to come into the open."[35] It is as though the living creatures are ordering the four horses and riders to go and do what they are going to do.

2. Fill in the chart below (6:1–8).

Horse	Color	Rider Description	Activity
#1	White	With bow, given a crown	Conquering conqueror
#2			
#3			
#4			

---

[35] Zodhiates, *Hebrew-Greek Key*, 1627

Now, in light of the Lamb opening the seals, the living creatures giving the command to "come!", and the repeated use of terms such as "given" and "permitted," who is ultimately in control? Who has authority over the chaos these horses and rider bring on planet earth? _____!

Though obvious, the generation that actually experiences the events associated with the seals may need to be reminded of this—that God *is* in control. The breaking of each individual seal will bring about prescribed, foretold events.

Recall Matthew 24:5–7 below.

"For many will come in my name, saying 'I am the Christ' and they will lead many astray. And you will hear of wars and rumors of wars, see that you are not alarmed for this must take place, but the end is not yet. For nation will rise against nation, and kingdom against kingdom, and there will be famines and earthquakes in various places." (See also Mark 13:5–8; Luke 21:8–13.)

Jesus foretold these events in His Olivet Discourse, but we weren't privy to what was transpiring in heaven to precipitate them. As we read and study the events associated with the breaking of the seals on that scroll, we are actually just reviewing all we learned in Matthew 24, Mark 13, and Luke 21. Now we get a glimpse of the heavenly drama that transpires to facilitate the drama on earth.

With the first seal, many false christs and the ultimate Antichrist come onto the stage of human history. With the second seal, wars are increased throughout the world. With the third seal, famine and economic collapse are rampant. With the fourth seal, a quarter of the world's population dies from the effects of the first three seals as well as resultant starvation, disease, and even wild beasts.

The events of the end of this age will take place over a seven-year period. This chunk of time was foretold in Daniel 9:24–27 and as such is referred to as "Daniel's seventieth week." But the events of the four horses and their riders comprise only the first three and a half years of that time period, the tribulation. As bad as things get, Jesus referred to them as just the "beginning of birth pains" (Matthew 24:8).

3. Read Revelation 6:9–11. With the opening of the fifth seal, the scene changes from earth to heaven. We are given a rare glimpse into the perspective heaven's occupants have regarding things taking place on earth. In this passage, we aren't told how the fifth seal affects earth. Jesus already told us that in His Olivet Discourse (Matthew 24:9–28).

When Jesus opens the fifth seal, who does John see (6:9–11)?

The s_____ of those who had been s_____ for the w_____ of God and w_____ they had borne.

4. Where are they?

U_____ the altar.

5. What question are they crying out to God?

How long before you will j_____ and a_____ our blood on those who d_____ on the e_____?

6. These souls are given white robes, and then what are they told to do?

R_____ a l_____ longer.

7. God tells them to rest until something has been completed. What is it?

a. Until the tribulation has been completed
b. Until the wrath of God has been completed
c. Until the full complement of fellow servants and brothers are killed as the slain were

This is not an easy text. A face-value reading of verse 11 states that there are indeed a previously set, limited, prescribed number of martyrs, and the ultimate judging and avenging (His wrath) that God will bring will *not occur* until that number is complete.

The fifth seal marks the beginning of the great tribulation. It coincides with increased martyrdom of the saints when the abomination of desolation is revealed in the middle of the seventieth week. How do we know that? Daniel said the abomination of desolation would break his covenant in the middle of the seven years, and Jesus said that is when the martyrdom will increase to an intensity never before seen.

Again, recall Matthew 24:9–22 below (also Mark 13:9–23; Luke 21:12–24) for Christ's description

Then they will deliver you up to tribulation and put you to death, and you will be hated by all nations for my name's sake. And then many will fall away and betray one another and hate one another. And many false prophets will arise and lead many astray. And because lawlessness will be increased, the love of many will grow cold. So when you see the abomination of desolation spoken of by the prophet Daniel, standing in the holy place (let the reader understand) then … flee … For then there will be great tribulation such has not been from the beginning of the world until now, no, and never will be. If those days had not been cut short, no human being would be saved … For false christs and false prophets will arise … so as to lead astray, if possible, even the elect.

8. From the above condensation of the Olivet Discourse as well as verses from Mark 13 and Luke 21, list the events on earth that result from the breaking of the fifth seal in heaven. Your list will be upsetting but real.

Here is our list:

As the number of martyrs is indeed being completed on earth, the love of many will have grown cold as lawlessness increases. Family members will betray one another, apparently turning in believers who will *not* pledge allegiance to the Antichrist, causing them to be killed. The Antichrist, the abomination of desolation, will set himself up in the holy place, and those in Jerusalem are to flee. The opening of the fifth seal will begin what Jesus calls a great tribulation upon earth such has never been or will be. In fact, if the time is not cut short, as Jesus explained will occur (Matthew 24:22) no one will survive.

9. Now we will see how God cuts short this time of the worst tribulation in history. Read Revelation 6:12–16.

We have come to the opening of the sixth seal. After it is opened, there will still be one seal left unbroken. Therefore, the scroll itself isn't yet unrolled. The breaking of the seventh seal and the opening of the scroll won't happen until the beginning of chapter 8.

The scene changes back to earth when Jesus opens the sixth seal. The events associated with it are catastrophic and worldwide.

10. List them.

    a. Great e_____
    b. S_____ black as sackcloth
    c. M_____ like blood
    d. S_____ … fell to earth like figs in a gale.
    e. S_____ vanished like a scroll rolled up.
    f. Every m_____ and i_____ removed from its place

All this was prophesied in Joel 2:30–31. "And I will show wonders in the heavens and on the earth, blood and fire and columns of smoke. The sun shall be turned to darkness, and the moon to blood, before the great and awesome day of the Lord comes."

In the first recorded sermon in church history, Peter quoted the above verses from Joel (Acts 2:17–21 emphasis added). "And in the last days it shall be, God declares, that I will pour out my spirit on all flesh … the sun shall be turned to darkness and the moon to blood, *before* the day of the Lord comes, the great and magnificent day."

Recall Matthew 24:29–30. "Immediately after the tribulation of those days, the sun will be darkened, and the moon will not give its light, and then stars will fall from heaven, and the powers of the heavens will be shaken. Then will appear in heaven the sign of the Son of Man, and then all the tribes of the earth will mourn, and they will see the Son of Man coming on the clouds of heaven with power and great glory."

When Jesus opens that sixth seal on the scroll in heaven, the cosmos is affected catastrophically. Jesus tells us this will occur immediately after the terrible tribulation and just before the coming of the Son of Man. Joel told us this will happen immediately before the day of the Lord. Sandwiched between those events, God turns out the heavenly lights, signaling the end of one and the beginning or coming of the other. No wonder all the tribes of the earth will mourn.

11. Read Revelation 6:15–17 to put all these layers of information together.
    What is the collective reaction of the most powerful on earth as well as the lowliest?

    They h_____ themselves in c_____ and among the rocks of the m_____, calling "F_____ on us and h_____ us."

12. From whom and what do they want to be hidden (6:16–17)?

    The f_____ of him who is seated on the t_____ and from the w_____ of the Lamb.

From the mightiest to the least, people would rather be buried alive, trapped in the rubble of the terrible earthquakes and crushed under the mountains than to face the Lord. Jesus said all the earth would mourn. Their world will seem to be falling apart with the breaking of that sixth seal.

13. Why are they so afraid (6:17)?

    For the great day of their w_____ has come and who can s_____?

The sixth seal has been broken, and soon the scroll will unroll; the day of the Lord's wrath is about to come upon the earth, and they are correct. No one can stand.

But there is hope. Those in Christ aren't appointed to His wrath. Recall Matthew 24:30–31.

"All the tribes of the earth will mourn and they will see the Son of Man coming … And He will send out His angels with a loud trumpet call, and they will gather His elect from the four winds."

14. Yes, all the tribes of the earth will mourn, but whom does Christ send His angels to gather?

His e_____.

There is no mention of this rescue in Revelation 6. Here in Revelation, we see only the response of the lost to the horrible wrath that is about to commence. They would rather be crushed under the mountains than face Him. The dichotomous reaction to the return of Christ is clearly seen in these two texts—fear and horror for those not in Christ and rescue and praise for those who are.

Note

Rapture positions are based on how the seals are viewed. If the events associated with the breaking of the seals are indeed the wrath of God, then the rapture must take place before they are broken. However, if the seals describe the tribulation and great tribulation that precede the wrath of God, beginning with the opening of the scroll, then the rapture wouldn't need to take place until just before the scroll is opened. According to those who beg the mountains to fall on them at the end of chapter 6, the wrath of God hasn't begun until then.

If the seals aren't the wrath of God but instead comprise the events of the tribulation and the great tribulation, then believers could be present for that. And though the tribulation, the first four seals, occupies the first half of the seven years, the great tribulation, which begins at the midpoint when persecution by the Antichrist increases, is cut short. The wrath of God, the day of the Lord, would then complete the allotted seven years. His wrath is much worse than even the great tribulation, but by His grace, His church is rescued before it begins by His gathering of His own.

Answer Key: 7. c

CHAPTER 39

INTERMISSION BEFORE THE SCROLL IS OPENED. REVELATION 7

We are now in uncharted territory. Whereas chapter 6 was a review of the events Jesus had prepared His followers for, as seen from a heavenly vantage point, chapter 7 is an intermission of sorts. The seventh seal is about to be opened in chapter 8, but there is a group of people on earth and a newly arrived, uncountable group in heaven that must first be considered before the wrath of the Lamb begins.

1. Read 7:1–8. Four angels are mentioned standing at the four corners of the earth. What are they doing (7:1)?

    Holding back the four w_____ of the earth that no w_____ might b_____ on earth or sea or against any t_____.

What have they been given power to do (7:2)?

    H_____ the earth and sea and trees.

Another angel rises from the east, having the seal of God with him, and he orders the others not to harm the earth until some people have been sealed [for their protection from the wrath as we will see later].

    How many people? _____,_____ (7:4)
    How many from each of the twelve tribes? (7:5-8)
    _____,_____

Note

The tribes of Dan and the half tribe of Ephraim aren't mentioned; there are various opinions by scholars as to why, but also note that Joseph essentially got a double allotment, one for himself and one for his son, Manasseh.

In chapter 9, we will see that these sealed ones aren't affected by the fifth trumpet, but otherwise, no more is said of these one hundred forty-four thousand until chapter 14, when we see these Jewish men following the Lamb wherever He goes, the firstfruits for God and for the Lamb. Because of this, the vast majority of scholars believe these sealed Jewish men are essentially one hundred forty-four thousand instantly saved witnesses witnessing to others, especially Jews, and encouraging them to trust Christ for salvation *during* the wrath of God, the day of the Lord.

Let's pause here and imagine what the world is like at this moment in the future. War, famine, plague, and even wild beasts have killed one-fourth of the world's population during the three and a half years of tribulation.

Then, with the beginning of the great tribulation, the Antichrist sets himself up in an apparently rebuilt temple as the abomination that makes the temple desolate, putting an end to the sacrifices that will have apparently been restarted there. He proclaims himself to be God and, as we will see, requires everyone to worship him *and* take his mark—or be killed. So much persecution of believers ensues that the souls under the altar in heaven cry out to God to ask, "How much longer?"

After the previously determined number of martyrs is completed, God intervenes in a mighty way and cuts short the great tribulation, and the world seems to fall apart—the sun, moon, and stars are dark; and every mountain and island is moved. The unsaved powerful as well as the lowly try to hide from the wrath of the Lamb when Jesus comes in the clouds. The saved dead come with Him, rise from the earth, and are transformed into new immortal bodies. The saved living are caught up and changed with them in the air to be immortal and perfected, all joining Jesus forever. The lost world watches this, terrified and desperately trying to make sense of it all.

And now … total stillness. The air is not even moving. Those left behind, terrified and in hiding, who would rather have been buried alive now slowly peek their heads out, wondering at the perfect, deadly calm.

They don't understand that it's a heavenly delay, a taking care of business, a sealing of one hundred forty-four thousand Jewish men, a remnant to be left on the earth during the day of the Lord.

The wrath of the Lamb is about to commence, and the newly (apparently saved) one hundred forty-four thousand have to be protected to endure it; as we learned in the Old Testament prophets, God always has a remnant.

After this event on earth, we have a scene change, and John is observing a coinciding event … in heaven.

2. Read Revelation 7:9–12.
   What does John see standing before the throne and the Lamb (7:9)?

   A great m_____ that no one could n_____ from every n_____ … t_____ … p_____ and l_____.

What are they wearing?

   W_____ robes. (This sort of makes all our concerns about our wardrobe seem trivial, doesn't it?)

What are they crying out in loud voices (7:10)?

   S_____ belongs to our G_____ who sits on the t_____ and to the L_____.

(The fact that salvation belongs to God should give us such assurance; it isn't ours to earn or deserve, nor is it ours to lose. It is a gift of grace He gives and never snatches away.)

When the uncountable multitude shouts this, what posture do the angels, elders, and living creature take? (7:11)

   "…they f_____ on their f_____…and worshiped God. (If it is ~~possible for you, try this right now—bow on your face and worship Him.~~)

What do they say as they worship? What do they ascribe to the Lord (7:12)?

   B_____ and g_____ and w_____ and t_____ and h_____ and p_____ and m_____ be to our God forever and ever! Amen.

3. Read Revelation 7:13–14. Here we read about a humorous encounter between John and one of the elders. The elder asks John the question we are wondering. Who are these people, and where did they come from? It will be seen that the elder knows the answer but asks John anyway, and John has no idea. Recall that at the time John was recording

Revelation, there were at most several thousand believers on the earth—a countable number. But now he is looking at a multitude no one can even count and respectfully replies to the elder, "Sir, you know."

In 7:14, the elder clearly explains that they are those who have come out of the ... "g_____ t_____."

As the poetry that follows demonstrates, they have suffered, experienced hunger and thirst, and endured scorching heat. They had great reason to weep, but now they are protected and provided for and comforted by the Lamb.

We, the authors, believe this multitude is the rescued, raptured church as well as all the saints throughout the ages—all who belong to Him. Some believe these are those left behind at the rapture who come to a saving faith during the day of the Lord. Whichever group they are, they worship.

CHAPTER 40

THE SEVENTH SEAL IS BROKEN AND FOUR TRUMPETS ARE BLOWN. REVELATION 8

1. Read 8:1–5. Chapter 8 opens with a most solemn ceremony. Jesus opens the seventh seal. For perhaps the only time in heavenly history, something happens in heaven … for half an hour. What is it?

   S_____.

Read chapter 4 again. There has been the sound of praise and power in heaven forever, but now something so immense is about to occur that there is silence. It seems an anticipatory reverence, fitting and heavily poignant, before the trumpets are blown and the great and dreadful wrath of the Lamb begins.

Next, the seven angels are given their seven trumpets, but a ceremony of prayer occurs prior to their blowing them.

2. Read 8:3–5 and sketch the scene, perhaps using cartoon-like blocks to show the progression of the action.

Where are your prayers and those of all the saints before you? Look where the smoke went. They are kept and offered with incense, and their smoke rises before God as a lovely aroma. Now with thunder and an earthquake, the silence is over, and it's time to blow the first four trumpets. The seals affected quarters of the world's population, the seven trumpets affect thirds, and the seven bowls to follow will affect all that remains.

In the Old Testament, trumpets were used to call God's people to Himself (think of Mt. Sinai) and to go to war (think of Jericho). With the trumpets of Revelation, He has called His people to Himself, and now His wrath will commence. Recall Matthew 24:31 and 1 Thessalonians 4:16; there will be a loud trumpet call when He gathers His elect to Himself, and then He will begin His day, the day of the Lord, His wrath.

3.   Read 8:6–12 and fill in the chart below.

Trumpet	1	2	3	4
Action	Hail and fire with blood			
Effect	One-third of earth and trees burned, including all grass			

4.   Though only one-third of the trees and earth are burned at this point, how much grass is burned up (8:7)?

A_____.

Recall 2 Peter 3:7 and imagine all the earth's grass burning. "The heavens and earth that now exist are stored up for fire being kept until the day of judgment."

Now, imagine the stench as one-third of the sea's creatures die (8:9) and the chaos as one-third of all the vessels on the oceans are destroyed.

Next, imagine one-third of all the fresh water on earth being bitter and undrinkable (8:10). Then picture the darkness or the dimming to one-third their normal power of the sun, moon, and stars (8:12). Think of the chaos and confusion on the earth. This is only the beginning stage of the wrath of God.

How long do each of these four trumpets last? Do their effects come and then ease up on the world before the next one begins? What is the Antichrist doing during these trumpets?

We aren't told the answers to these questions. We can only use our imaginations and realize that the one hundred forty-four thousand and the two witnesses at the temple (chapter 11) continue to proclaim God's truth. We can only imagine and pray. Surely these events will get the attention of some, and they will trust Christ.

5.   Now we come to a pause. Just as the first four seals were something of a preamble to the horror that the fifth and sixth seals brought, the first four trumpets are mild in comparison to what is about to come upon the earth.

An unusual messenger gives the warning. John sees and hears something flying directly over him. What is it (8:13)?

A talking e_____.

What does the eagle say regarding the coming effects of the next three trumpets on those who dwell on the earth?

W_____ w_____w_____.

As if the first four trumpets hadn't been catastrophic enough.

CHAPTER 41

THE FIFTH AND SIXTH TRUMPETS ARE BLOWN. REVELATION 9

The eagle was right. The next trumpets are unimaginably worse.

1. Read 9:1–6 and sketch in comic-book style the movement, events, and creatures associated with the fifth trumpet.

Where had the locusts been kept (9:1-3)?

In the b_____ p_____.

What kind of power do they have (9:5)?

To sting like a s_____.

2. Now read 9:7–12 and draw and label a locust. Imagine that face.

The torment of their stinging will be so bad that people will long to die but will not be able to.

How long does their torment last (9:5)?

___ months

This is the only specific time duration we are given for any of the seals, trumpets, or bowls. The fifth trumpet lasts five months.

The actual location of these locusts' holding place, the bottomless pit (or abyss), is unknown, but that doesn't make it imaginary. It is mentioned several times in Revelation, and it was the place where the demons did *not* want to go to when Jesus cast them into the pigs instead (Luke 8:31–32). The bottomless pit is so bad that even demons don't want to be in there. As we will see in Revelation 11, it is also the place where the beast (the Antichrist) has been kept.

3. The pit has a king. He is specifically named in both Hebrew and Greek. What are those names (9:11)?

   A_____ and A_____.

This fallen angel's name refers to destruction and the one who destroys. These names are found in mythology. Could it be the myths of old were real? Demonically real?

4. The terrible locusts are the result of the fifth trumpet or first "woe" (9:12). The sixth trumpet is blown, and the second "woe" begins.

Read 9:13–16. A voice from the golden altar in heaven tells the angel who blew the trumpet to release the four angels, who are bound at the Euphrates River. Since they are bound and need to be released, they are quite possibly *fallen* angels. The timing of their release is very specific, down to the hour. These horrific plagues are previously ordained and all under the control of God.

5. What is the number of their mounted troops, who will kill one-third of mankind?

   Do the math: 10,000 X 10,000 X 2 =_____

Those are *a lot* of demonic troops. But remember, the number of those worshipping the Lamb was innumerable.

6. Read 9:17–19. Sketch and label the horses and the troops. (You may want to use colored pencils so you can more fully imagine two hundred million of these creatures.)

7. How do they kill (9:17)?

By "f_____ and s_____ and s_____ coming out of their mouths." Not to mention the wounding they inflict with their tails.

Let us again take a moment to ponder and discuss your sketches. Consider the terrifying horror the creatures of trumpets five and six will bring. Someday this will actually happen.

8. However, notice again who is in charge, who is in control.

In 9:1, the fallen star, either Satan or a high-order demon, has to be g_____ the key to the shaft.
In 9:3, the locusts are g_____ power.
In 9:4, they are told what and whom they can and *cannot* harm.

9. Who *are* they allowed to harm (9:4)?

Those "who do not have the s_____ of God on the f_____."

10. Who *does* have the seal of God on their foreheads (Revelation 7:3)?

The _____,_____.

The wrath of God does *not* harm His chosen ones. The one hundred forty-four thousand Jewish men from designated tribes will be His witnesses by their testimony *and* by their being impervious to the locusts.

This is what the wrath of God looks like. This is what our sin deserves. Have you ever been more thankful for your salvation by His grace and for His mercy toward us? We don't need to suffer what we deserve in our flesh. This knowledge is a powerful motivator for sharing the gospel even more fervently.

And yet in 9:20–21 we see the reaction of the world, those who survive the plagues. The events of the sixth trumpet will occur somewhere close to the end of the seventieth week. Those who survive these plagues have been through the events of all seven seals and the first six trumpets.

11. Read 9:20–21. What is the attitude of those not killed by the plagues? Circle all that apply.

a. They repent and worship God.
b. They don't repent of the works of their hands.
c. They fall on their faces before God and plead for His mercy.
d. They don't give up their worship of idols and demons.
e. They don't repent of their murders, sorceries, sexual immoralities, and thefts.

The question is often asked, "When is the last call of grace? When is the last chance to be saved?" They could plead for mercy; they could repent, but they do not. It isn't stated, but judging from the hardness of the hearts of those left alive after the sixth trumpet, it would seem that there is no more salvation at this point. We can rest in the fact that God is to be trusted with salvation; anyone who is going to be saved will be saved.

Before we move on to chapter 10, let us pause and take stock of who is on the earth and what the earth will be like at this point. The sixth trumpet is probably sounded very near the end of the seven years.

First, there will be fewer people. The population will have been reduced by one-quarter with the opening of the first four seals. Then many believers will have been martyred with the fifth seal in the middle of the seventieth week. Then all believers who survived will have been evacuated upon the return of Christ. In association with the catastrophic events of the sixth seal, there will be many more deaths.

When the scroll is unrolled, the fires and waters affected by the first four trumpets will kill many, and now one-third of those left are dead by the plagues of the two hundred million demonic horse or lion troops.

12. So, who *is* on the earth at this point? List the groups you can think of. You will find our list below.

1. There are the one hundred forty-four thousand saved and sealed Jewish men.
2. There are those who presumably come to faith in Christ by their witness.
3. There is the Antichrist and the false prophet.
4. There are all those who have taken the mark of the beast; though many also have died, those still living are hardened and evil.
5. Then there is a group of Jews who won't bow to the Antichrist but haven't yet trusted Christ. We will see this group in chapter 12.
6. There are the two witnesses we will read of in chapter 11.
7. There is perhaps another group, non-believing, non-Jewish survivor types, some who hide and stay under the radar of the Antichrist while not taking his mark. This seems unlikely due to the nature of the mark of the beast and his image, which we will read about in chapter 13, but perhaps some will escape and hopefully trust Christ in the end.

CHAPTER 42

AN INTERLUDE, A PRIVATE CEREMONY. REVELATION 10

Chapter 10 is best seen as an interlude before the seventh trumpet is blown. Just as we saw an interlude in chapter 7 before the seventh seal was broken, some things must be explained, and a ceremony must take place before that last trumpet is sounded. Also, the second woe, the full complement of the sixth trumpet events hasn't yet passed. We won't see closure of the second woe until Revelation 11:14.

In the meantime, chapter 10 depicts a solemn, momentous ceremony. It is a very private ceremony; only John and the Mighty Angel are present.

1.   Read 10:1–7 and sketch what John sees.

2.   Who is this Mighty Angel?

     a.   Jesus
     b.   The strong angel of chapter 5
     c.   The Angel of the Lord
     d.   We don't know for sure.

Many scholars say he is Jesus because of his great authority; the description of his face, legs, and voice; and the rainbow over his head.

3. What does this Mighty Angel proclaim, actually raising His right hand and swearing by God (10:6)?
That there would be no more d_____.

4. Delay of what?

   a. Of the mystery of God being fulfilled
   b. Of the seven thunders being sealed
   c. Of the little scroll being opened

The Mighty Angel announces that at the next trumpet to be sounded, the seventh and last, the mystery of God would be fulfilled; all the prophecies would be complete, finished, fulfilled.

The Greek word for "mystery" is *mysterion*,[36] "a divine secret or sacred profundity." Paul wrote in Romans 11:25 and Ephesians 3:3 of the mystery of the previously unknown inclusion of Gentiles into God's family. Using scripture to comment on scripture, we see that this mystery, like God's plan to include Gentiles, is something previously unknown and not understood, but it is now made known and completed with the blowing of the seventh trumpet.

5. A voice from heaven tells John to take the little, open scroll from the Mighty Angel who stands on the land and sea. What does the Mighty Angel tell him to do with it (10:9)?

   a. Eat the scroll.
   b. Prophesy about peoples and nations.
   c. Seal the scroll.

6. What does the scroll taste like?

   a. Bitter herbs
   b. Sweet honey

7. How did John feel when he ate it.

   a. Happy because evil people were getting what they deserved
   b. It made his stomach bitter.

8. Why do you think the scroll was at first sweet but then made his stomach bitter?

_____.

Some scholars say the little open scroll is the previously sealed and now-opened scroll containing the trumpets. Others say it is the coming bowl judgments.

---

[36] Zodhiates, *Hebrew-Greek Key*, 1652

This isn't definitively stated in the text. Whatever it is, vengeance and justice seem sweet at first. But the sorrow, the bitterness of seeing, as Jonathan Edwards said in "Sinners in the Hands of an Angry God,"[37] makes John physically ill.

Answer Key: 2. d
                4. a
                5. a
                6. b
                7. b

---

[37] Wikipedia.org/wiki>Sinners_in_the_Hands/Jonathan Edwards/last edited August, 16,2020

CHAPTER 43

THE TWO WITNESSES AND THE SEVENTH TRUMPET. REVELATION 11

Whereas chapter 10 was an interlude and ceremony, and seems to take place at the end of the seven years, chapter 11:1–14 may be seen as a *meanwhile*. Meanwhile, back in the middle of the seven years when the fifth seal was broken, a temple was mentioned. (That coincides exactly with when Jesus and Paul mentioned the temple, when the abomination of desolation or man of lawlessness appeared there.)

1. Read 11:1–3. John is given a measuring rod and told to measure three things (measurement connotes ownership and guardianship). What three things is he to measure?

   a. The outer court
   b. The temple
   c. The worshippers
   d. The city wall
   e. The altar

2. He is told *not* to measure the outer court (11:2) because it is …

   g_____ over to the n_____ and they will t_____ the holy city.

Recall Luke 21:20–24. "But when you see Jerusalem surrounded by armies, then know that its desolation has come near. Then let those who are in Judea flee to the mountains … Jerusalem will be trampled underfoot by the Gentiles, until the times of the Gentiles are fulfilled."

Jesus told us armies would surround Jerusalem and that Gentiles (the nations, non-Jews) would trample them underfoot when the great tribulation began until the times of the Gentiles were fulfilled. Revelation 11:2 is almost a word-for-word quotation of this passage.

Jesus warns those in Jerusalem to flee to the mountains because the desolation is near; this is the same warning he gives in Matthew 24 and Mark 13 when the abomination that makes it all desolate appears. This occurs in the middle of Daniel's seventieth week.

Recall Daniel 9:27 (NIV). "He will confirm a covenant with many for one seven. In the middle of the seven, he will put an end to sacrifice and offering. And on a wing of the temple, he will set up an abomination that causes desolation, until the end that is decreed is poured out on him."

3. How long will the holy city (Jerusalem) be given over to the nations (Revelation 11:2)?

_____ months.

(Note the repetition of the same time allotment seen over and over in Revelation.)

Now, you are probably wondering about the temple John is instructed to measure. The scene takes place on earth at the middle of the seventieth week. At the time of the writing of this study, there is no temple in Jerusalem, and there are no sacrifices being offered by priestly, religious Jews. The Temple Mount has been called the most valuable thirty-six acres of real estate on earth, and it is presently occupied by two Muslim sites.

In 2009, a group called The Temple Mount and Land of Israel Faithful[38] brought a thirteen-ton cornerstone through the Jaffa Gate and into the Old City in preparation for the rebuilding of the temple. Whenever they have attempted to actually get onto the Temple Mount itself, riots have resulted. For the sacrificial system to be reinstated and then halted by the Antichrist in the middle of the seventieth week, there must be a temple. It may be a tabernacle–style temple, much smaller that the Solomonic or Herodian temples, but there must be a temple with the sacrificial altar and all the accompanying furniture, vestments, trumpets, implements, ashes, and so forth for religious Jews to offer the sacrifices. The Temple Institute in the Jewish Quarter of the Old City has everything ready. When we visited, they told us they are ready the moment they are able to get on the Temple Mount. Many of those in the Levitical lineage know their DNA, and a specific marker has been shown to be linked with the priestly line.[39]

We Christians know Jesus was the final sacrifice for sin once and for all time. When He cried out, "It is finished!" on the cross, the sacrificial system was finished. However, many religious

---

[38] https://www.google.com./templemountfaithfl.org./Temple Mount and Land of Israel Faithful Movement/1997-2020

[39] Google.com/sciencedaily.com/priestly gene shared by widely dispersed jews/July 14, 1998

Jews don't *know* Christ and His sacrificial death in our place. Scripture is clear that there will be sacrifices the Antichrist will terminate. In His providence, God will use the Jews to orchestrate the events of His Son's coming to earth for the second time.

We can only speculate about these events, but we know it will be under God's control and in His timing. A charismatic leader, later known as the Antichrist, may negotiate what has heretofore been impossible and allow the temple to be rebuilt, perhaps sharing the mount with the Muslim sites. Sacrifices will resume only for him to cause them to cease after the first three and a half years. At that point, he will be totally empowered by Satan, and the abomination of his presence will desolate the temple (spoken of in Daniel 9:27)

4. Read Revelation 11:3–7. Here we are introduced to two new players in this narrative, and we are informed of the entire extent of their ministry. How long will the two witnesses prophesy under God's authority? (11:3)

   _____days.

The Lord repeatedly makes the exact duration of these events plain. The city is trampled for forty-two months, and the two witnesses prophecy for 1,260 days.

5. Using a Jewish thirty-day month, forty-two months = _____ days or three and a half years. His limits and His desire for us to be precisely informed demonstrate His grace and His intimate knowledge of us.

How do we know He is speaking of the *last* three-and-one-half-year period and not the first? Skip ahead to 11:14. The events of the second woe (the sixth trumpet) are completed at the point when the witnesses have completed their 1,260-day stint on earth. That happens at the end of the seventieth week, and it all began when the desolation of Jerusalem began, which happened in the middle of the seventieth week.

In fact, all references to time in Revelation refer to this particular time chunk—the *last* three and one half years (a time, times, and half a time), forty-two months, or 1260 days. Surprisingly, though the number seven is used repeatedly throughout the book, it is never used regarding the seven years we think of as the last days. Only the last half is specified numerically. We get the seven-year delineation from Daniel 9—the last *seven* or week of years of the seventy apportioned weeks.

6. What powers do the witnesses have?

   If anyone would harm them, f_____ p_____ from their mouth and c_____ their foes … They have the power to s_____ the s_____ … power over the waters to turn them into b_____ and to strike the earth with every kind of p_____.

They are God's two witnesses, who prophesy and testify, indestructible until they are finished.

Who are they? There is much speculation among scholars as to their identities. Many, if not most, believe them to be Moses and Elijah for several reasons. Their powers are similar to the old prophets, shutting the sky and bringing about plagues. They were the two who showed up with Him on the Mount of Transfiguration, and they both had unusual deaths—Elijah was taken in a chariot of fire, and Moses died alone with God and was buried by Him.

The text doesn't say, but as these two witnesses proclaim God's truth during the great tribulation, through the return of Christ, and then through the wrath of God (the events comprising the second half of the seventieth week), perhaps some come to faith. Recall Malachi 4:5. "Behold I will send you Elijah the prophet before the great and awesome day of the Lord comes. And he will turn the hearts of fathers to their children and the hearts of children to their fathers, lest I come and strike the land with a decree of utter destruction." If indeed one of the witnesses is Elijah, this would be when that prophecy is fulfilled, and those fathers and children who are reconciled are perhaps also reconciled to God through Christ.

7. Where are they located?

    a. Rome
    b. Egypt
    c. Sodom
    d. Jerusalem

Based on the immediate context regarding the temple and that they are killed where their Lord was crucified, we can presume they are in Jerusalem. Recall that the book (scroll) of Revelation was circulated among the seven churches, and much of it was coded for protection of the recipients if intercepted. It is one of the reasons for its highly symbolic nature.

8. When are they killed (11:7)?

    When they have f_____ their testimony.

The Antichrist and his minions apparently make numerous attempts on their lives, trying to stop them from tormenting them with truth, only to be consumed. God doesn't allow them to be killed until they are finished.

9. Who kills them (11:7)?

    The b_____ that rises from the b_____ p_____.

This is the first mention of the character so prevalent in this narrative, the beast. We will shortly see that he is the Antichrist, but he is never called that in the book of Revelation. He is always referred to as the "beast" with the pronoun *it*. Notice also that the beast had been kept in the bottomless pit, the abyss (where even the demons didn't want to go), until it was God's time for him (it) to be on earth.

10. When the beast kills the two witnesses, how do those who dwell on the earth (the lost) react (11:9–10)?

For three and a half days they "gaze at their d_____ bodies … in the s_____ … and r_____ over them and make m_____ and exchange p_____(!) because (they) had been a t_____."

The earth dwellers hate hearing the truth proclaimed by these two so much that they give each other gifts upon their death. It may be that they blame the witnesses for the events of the sixth and seventh seals and the first six trumpet judgments, especially those locusts and troops of horse/lion creatures. All that is concurrent with their witness. The people think their source of torment has been defeated, and they make a holiday of their deaths. Oh, the depravity of mankind in our lost and fallen state.

11. But after three and a half days, they live again. Read and sketch in comic-book-style frames the scenes depicted in verses 11:9–13.

The two witnesses are called back up to heaven, and as they rise, their enemies watch in terror. (Perhaps the earthquake in Jerusalem is the same one described in Zechariah 14.) The text tells us that those who live (11:13) "gave glory to the God of heaven." Hopefully, some are saved because this certainly seems to be their last chance.

Now we come to the blowing of the seventh trumpet. The scene is set in heaven. We don't see the consequent events on earth when the seventh trumpet is blown, but we hear the voices in heaven.

12. Read 11:15–18. When the seventh trumpet is blown, what do the heavenly voices say?

"The kingdom of the w_____ has *become* the kingdom of our Lord and of His Christ and he shall reign f_____ and ever." Are you singing? We are! (emphasis added)

Recall that in chapter 10 Jesus said there would "be no more delay" when the seventh trumpet was blown. The time has come; every prophetic text in the Word of God is fulfilled. The unchallenged reign of the King of kings and Lord of lords has begun. The kingdom of the world has *become* the kingdom of our Lord.

Read verses 16–18 *aloud*. Though the saints and prophets are rewarded, there is a heaviness to the text; the dead are judged, and the destroyers are destroyed. Remember, the eagle said there were three woes; the seventh trumpet is glorious for believers but a woe for the unsaved.

13. Finally, in 11:19, we see an amazing thing. The temple in heaven is opened.

    Who or what is in it?

    a. Worshippers
    b. Jesus
    c. The ark of the covenant

The *real* ark of the covenant is the one Moses used as his prototype. But why do we glimpse the ark at this moment? The text doesn't explain. What do you think? The world has become His kingdom forever, and perhaps the purpose of the ark has been fulfilled at the blowing of the final trumpet.

SUMMARY THUS FAR

The Second Coming of Christ, like His first, consists of many events. It begins when He returns in the clouds, intervening to rescue His church just in time. He also translates all believers, dead and alive, into new, eternal, imperishable, immortal bodies at that same moment. Then He oversees the events of His wrath, the wrath of the Lamb, the day of the Lord. Those events are contained in the seven trumpets, and then the kingdom of this world *becomes* His kingdom in a way not realized before. It has always been His, but this moment ushers in a new era, as the text says, ("You have *taken* your great power and begun to reign" [11:17]), finally reigning physically and literally as well as spiritually.

CHAPTER 44

A WOMAN, A DRAGON, A WAR, AND A WILDERNESS. REVELATION 12

Maybe you are wondering, *But wait. We have eleven more chapters. What about those bowls? This is not yet over.* You are correct. There are many more layers of information for us to add to our understanding of the revealed glory of God.

So far, in chapters 5–11, the events have been revealed in a relatively chronological order with some interludes and "meanwhiles." In chapter 12, we step back and fly above our timeline to see the grander, vast array of the redemption story—from the beginning of time to the middle of the seventieth week. Chapters 12–14 give more layers of background and meanwhile information.

It will seem as though we will be covering time periods we have already covered. We will. God's Word is providing more information regarding some important and evil players—Satan, the Antichrist, and the false prophet. Satan will be kicked out of heaven at the middle of the seventieth week; furious, he will completely empower his Antichrist and the false prophet on earth. Then in chapter 15 we will attend another somber and beautiful ceremony, all before the terrible and cathartic bowls are poured on the earth in chapter 16.

Chapter 12 begins with an overview of a vast time span as seen from the heavenly perspective. We see the coming of the Savior and Satan's desire to destroy Him since the beginning.

1. Read 12:1–4. Sketch the scene below. Notice that the sign appeared in heaven. Your picture will be weird.

2. Who is the great red dragon? Read ahead to verse 9.

   S_____.

But who is the woman?

Our best understanding of these highly symbolic verses is as follows:

The woman is Israel, laboring throughout the centuries, a summation of her agonies throughout the entire Old Testament as she labored to bring about Messiah.

The dragon is definitely Satan, who desired to stop Messiah before He ever began; he stands before the woman, Israel, ready to devour her Son the moment He is born.

The stars of heaven are angels, one-third of which became the demonic force when Satan was cast from heaven at the dawn of time (Isaiah 14:12–16; Ezekiel 28:13–16).

The seven heads of the dragon with seven diadems may possibly represent the seven beast kingdoms that persecuted Israel throughout the course of history—Egypt, Assyria, Babylon, Media-Persia, Greece, Rome, and an as-yet-unknown seventh.

These few verses serve as a plausible explanation for Israel's vicissitudes throughout the ages. Satan's evil desire has been, and continues to be, to keep Israel from being used in the coming of the Messiah—both His first and second comings.

3. Read 12:5–6. The woman, Israel, gave birth to the One who would rule with a rod of iron (this is the fulfillment of the Messianic promise in Psalm 2). Then, in a rather confusing telescoping and condensation of time, we see Jesus returned to His throne in Heaven, and we find ourselves in the middle of the seventieth week with the *woman* fleeing, to be protected for 1,260 days.

Like a rock skipping over the water, we are told specific points of information that will be pertinent to our understanding of the rest of the chapter. Recall that Jesus warns those in Jerusalem, those who apparently refuse to worship the Antichrist, to flee when she is surrounded by armies and the abomination of desolation is in the temple. Now we know where they flee and exactly how long they are protected. They go to a place God prepared for them for the last half of the seventieth week, for 1,260 days.

4. Read 12:7–12. Here we read of something never before seen, a war in heaven. Who is fighting whom?

    M_____ and his angels against the d_____ and his angels (demons).
    Who is defeated? The d_____, who we know to be Satan.

To be sure we have no doubt as to his identity, list the other titles he is given within the text.

Ancient s_____. (Recall Genesis 3, the serpent in the garden of Eden.)
D_____.
D_____ of the whole _____.

Satan is cast down, along with his minions.

5. Where is he cast (Revelation 12:9)?

    a. To earth
    b. To hell
    c. To the bottomless pit

Until this point in time, in the middle of the seventieth week, though he was no longer an inhabitant of heaven, Satan has apparently had some type of access. Recall Job 1 and 2, and consider Ephesians 6:12. "For we do not wrestle against flesh and blood, but against the rulers, against the authorities, against the cosmic powers over this present darkness, against the spiritual forces of evil *in the heavenly places.*"(emphasis added). This is a mystery we don't understand.

6. Reread Revelation 12:10–12. Why is heaven now rejoicing?

    Because the "a_____ of our b_____ has been thrown down."
    Where had he been accusing the brethren?
    Before our G_____.
    How often has Satan been accusing us?
    D_____ and n_____ (constantly).

Apparently, until this monumental moment when Michael and his angels cast Satan out of heaven for good, Satan has had some sort of access to the throne. That evil, ancient accuser of the brethren has been accusing us day and night before God. It will not be until the middle of the last seven years of this age that he finally *stops* accusing us.

7. How do the brethren conquer Satan (12:11)?

    By the b_____ of the Lamb and by the word of their t_____ …
    even unto d_____.

Even unto death, the saints are victorious over Satan. Heaven is rejoicing because Satan no longer has access. The constant accusing that has deceived believers through the ages, ceases.

We wonder what this turn of events will do in the hearts of believers left alive on the earth. This will occur when the great tribulation begins in the middle of the seven years or seventieth week. Will believers be more empowered to face persecution and martyrdom because the accuser is no longer causing doubts and accusations of guilt and unworthiness? Pause here to ponder and discuss this.

_____

_____

_____

8. The devil is now operating under a new economy. His wrath is greater than at any time in history, because he knows something. What does he know (12:12)?

   That his time is s_____.

9. How short? Read 12:6, 13–17.

The woman, Israel (those Jews who won't worship the Antichrist), flees to a place where she is to be nourished for 1,260 days. Zechariah 14:2 actually says half of the city will go into exile. She flies away from that ancient serpent and is protected in the wilderness. This is the fulfillment of Jesus's instructions to those in Jerusalem to flee when they see the abomination of desolation. The abomination of desolation is seen at the middle of the seventieth week, leaving 1,260 days for her to be protected.

10. How are the 1,260 (12:6) days stated in another way (12:14)?

    "A t_____, t_____, and h_____ a time," thereby equating 1,260 days with three and a half years.

From the middle of the seventieth week, for the last three and a half years, 1,260 days, or forty-two months, Satan is *on* earth. His time is short, only 1,260 days. He will, as we will see, fully empower his anti-Messiah, and everything will change. Furious, he will try to drown the remnant of Israel, but God will intervene and protect her. Since Satan can't get to her, he stomps off to make war with the rest of her offspring.

11. Who are the rest of her offspring (12:17)?

    a. Those who keep the commandments
    b. Those who hold to the testimony of Jesus

Those who keep the commandments and hold to the testimony of Jesus are "the rest of her offspring." Satan is furious and stomps after those who belong to Jesus. As believers, our roots are in Israel, and our Savior is the Lion of the tribe of Judah.

And so begins the great tribulation. In chapter 12, we have seen the heavenly events that precipitate it. Michael has thrown Satan out of heaven for good. This may well be what is in view in Daniel 12:1. "At that time shall arise Michael, the great prince who has charge of your people. And there shall be a time of trouble such as never has been." If Michael is indeed the restrainer of 2 Thessalonians 2:6-7, this event coincides perfectly with the point at which he stops restraining. Satan is now on earth; and unable to destroy the protected remnant of Israel, he furiously pursues believers in Jesus. In chapter 13 we will see how he goes about this.

Answer Key: 5. a
                10. a, b

CHAPTER 45

TWO BEASTS: THE ANTICHRIST AND THE FALSE PROPHET. REVELATION 13

1. Read 13:1–2 and the last sentence of chapter 12. While Satan watches from the shore, a beast rises from the sea. Sketch and label this beast.

2. Now compare this beast to your sketch of the dragon in chapter 12.

   They each have (how many)_____ horns (symbolic of power).
   They each have (how many) _____heads (symbolic of kings and/or kingdoms).
   The dragon has diadems on his h_____.
   The beast has diadems on his h_____.

3. What do you think could be the significance of that?

   _____

   _____

4. What does the dragon give to the beast (Revelation 13:2)?

   a. His power
   b. His throne
   c. His sovereignty, omnipotence, and omniscience
   d. His great authority

Satan can give his beast his power, throne, and authority; but he is not sovereign, omnipotent, or omniscient.

It's no coincidence that the beast is likened to the leopard, bear, and lion. These, along with an indescribable horned beast, represent the beast empires of Daniel 7. This beast appears to be a composite of all those.

Though in chapter 11 we saw the end of the seven trumpets and the end of the seventieth week, much of chapters 12–14 are a "meanwhile"—layers of more information regarding events happening at the same time. This event, Satan fully empowering his protégé, seemingly a mimicking of the incarnation, will occur at the middle of the seventieth week. This would coincide with the breaking of the fifth seal and the beginning of the great tribulation. At this point, the charismatic leader and peacemaker of the first three and a half years, the rider of the white horse of the first seal, will be revealed for who he is—the anti-Messiah or Antichrist, the Satan man, the beast.

5. Read 13:3–4. Why does the whole (non-believing) earth marvel as they follow the beast (13:3)?

   Because one head seemed to have "a m_____ wound but its mortal wound was h_____." Satan is nothing but a cheap copy; he is endeavoring to build his own evil trinity with his *son*, having returned to life after a death-inflicting wound.

The world will buy it (13:4), and they will w_____ the dragon and his beast.

6. Read 13:5–8 to understand what the beast is given and allowed to do. Again, how long is the beast allowed to exercise authority and utter haughty blasphemy?

   _____ months (or 1,260 days or three and a half years).

7. Who will worship the beast (Antichrist), and who will not (13:7–8)? Fill in the chart and see our answers below.

   These Will Worship the Beast   **These Will Not Worship the Beast**

These Will Worship the Beast	These Will Not Worship the Beast
*All who dwell on the earth	
*Those who names were *not* written before the foundation of the world in the Lamb's book of life	*Those whose names *were* written in the Lamb's book of life before the foundation of the world

8. Will the beast be allowed to conquer the saints (13:7)?

    a. Yes
    b. No

Based on your answers to the above questions, what do you think will happen to believers who refuse to worship the beast? _____

9. Now, with greater understanding, read these seemingly obtuse verses: 13:9–10.

    What do you think these somber verses mean?

    a. There is an inevitability of prison and even martyrdom for some, and this will require great faith and endurance on the part of the saints.
    b. Satan is in charge of the prison system at this time.
    c. Gun control will be worldwide, and swords will be the method of execution.

We are learning more about the players who initiate and perpetrate the great tribulation on the believers in Jesus. Satan has been cast out of heaven to earth, where he uniquely empowers his anti-Messiah, who is the abomination of desolation. While the fifth seal has been broken (6:9), the martyrs under the altar in heaven ask God how much longer before their blood is avenged. They are told to wait until the full number of other martyrs is complete. In that light, these somber verses take on more meaning; there is an inevitability that many saints will be imprisoned, and some will lose their lives when they stand for their true Lord and Savior. It is no wonder that 13:10 closes with, "Here is a call for the endurance and faith of the saints."

10. Read 13:11–18. We are now introduced to the final player in this evil trinity, the false prophet. From where does it (the pronoun used in the text) rise?

    The e_____.

What animal does it resemble?

    A l_____ with two horns.

How does it speak?

Like a d_____.

It looks like a lamb but speaks like a dragon.

11. Make a listing of what this beast is allowed to do. Notice that it, like the first beast, is *allowed* to act. All of this is still under God's control.

Check your list here:

* It performs signs to deceive those on earth.
* It makes fire come from heaven.
* It tells earth dwellers to make an image for the beast.
* It gives breath to the image so it can speak and causes all who won't worship the image to be slain.
* It causes all, no matter their social standing, to need a mark on their right hand or forehead to buy or sell.

12. What does the mark consist of?

    a. The beast's name
    b. A pentagram
    c. The number of the beast's name, 666

says it will. Three times in this chapter the reader or hearer is advised to understand, to endure, to be wise, and to pay close attention. (See vv. 9–10 and 18.)

This time period, the great tribulation, will be horrendous for believers. They will be unable to buy food and essentials for their children because they won't take the mark. Believers will appear foolish, intolerant, and ignorant. The mark will be proclaimed as the answer to the world's problems. Terrorism, crime, lost children, medical and financial issues, and so forth will all be answered by the mark. Believers will seem to be the irresponsible troublemakers who won't go along.

13. Quickly skip ahead to 14:9–11 for the consequences of taking the mark and going along.

What are the consequences?

_____.

Do you now see the danger in thinking the church won't be on earth when Antichrist and his lackey come into power? We could mistakenly assume that that microchip or whatever is used could not possibly be the mark of the beast because believers won't be here for that. It will be so tempting to just go along for ease and comfort, for "peace and safety." But Satan, the beast, and his false prophet are the haters of your soul.

Praise God He cuts short this time period and rescues His church. Otherwise, there would be no believers left to rescue.

Answer Key: 4. a, b, d
                  8. a
                  9. a
                12. a,

THE ONE HUNDRED FORTY-FOUR THOUSAND, THREE ANGELS, AND TWO HARVESTS, REVELATION 14

After learning of all the horror and havoc the two beasts would be allowed to wreak on earth, we come to another "meanwhile chapter." The scenes depicted in this chapter can best be taken as three separate vignettes, which take place while the Antichrist and false prophet are empowered by Satan and allowed to work.

1. Read 14:1–5. First, we see what becomes of the one hundred forty-four thousand, to whom we were introduced in chapter 7. A powerful, heavenly voice sings a *new* song before the throne of God that only the one hundred forty-four thousand can learn.

They are called "firstfruits for God and the Lamb." In the Old Testament, the Festival of Firstfruits was at the beginning of the barley harvest, heralding a promise of more to come. In 1 Corinthians 15:20, Paul called Jesus our firstfruits as the first to be resurrected from the dead, thus ensuring our resurrection (and just as He was our Passover ... Passover, He indeed rose from the grave on the day when the Festival of Firstfruits was celebrated). Based on that understanding, why do you think this unique group of sealed, Jewish men from each of the twelve tribes is referred to as "firstfruits"?

_____

_____

There will be more—more to come. More people will trust Christ during the terrible time of the wrath of the Lamb because of this unique group's witness.

2. Read 14:6–11. The first angel proclaims the gospel. To whom does he proclaim it (14:6)?

To e_____ nation, tribe, language, and people.

What does he say (14:7)?

F_____ God and give Him g_____ … and w_____ Him.

Why does he say that?

Because the hour of His j_____ has c_____.

God has commissioned us as humans to share the gospel. We have had that privilege since His church began. But here He uses an angel. Could this be how Matthew 24:14 (in which all the world hears the gospel before the end) is finally fulfilled? We can only speculate, but we can be assured that everyone will hear it.

3. The second angel (14:8) declares that Babylon the Great, who made the nations drink of sexual immorality, is fallen. By what pronoun is Babylon referred to?

   a. He
   b. She
   c. It

This is the first mention of Babylon in Revelation, but we will read much more of her in chapters 16–18. We will also see in chapter 19 that heaven rejoices at her fall.

It is commonly understood that Babylon represents, as she has from the time of the tower of Babel, false religion and spiritual (as well as sexual) adultery. And her doom is sure.

4. The third angel (14:9–11) follows the others with that solemn, horrific warning you recorded in chapter 13. Once again, what happens if one takes the mark and worships the beast and its image?

   He will d_____ the wine of God's w_____ … and be t_____ with f_____ and s_____ in the presence of the holy a_____ and … the L_____.

5. How long does the torment last?

   a. Ten days
   b. Three and a half years
   c. Forty-two months
   d. Forever and ever

It's difficult to read of the judgment of God, but it's just and true.

6. Go back and read what happens to those who *refuse* to take the mark and worship the beast in Revelation 13:15. They will "be s_____."

Either death of this body and eternity with Christ or eternal torment … choose this day whom you will serve. No wonder Revelation 14:12–13 reads as it does; this *does* call for endurance of the saints, and God gives a particularly sweet blessing for those who die because of Him in this terrible time. Now to the third and final vignette of chapter 14.

7. Read Revelation 14:14–20. Here we see two harvests: one (14:15) because "the harvest of the earth is fully ripe" and one in which the grape harvest of the earth is thrown into the "winepress of the wrath of God" (14:19).

This highly symbolic text is difficult, and many scholars differ on the meaning. It possibly represents the rapture harvest followed by the judgment of the wicked. Or it could represent the harvest of those saved *during* the day of the Lord, followed by a judgment harvest. These harvests may be related to the sheep and goat judgment of Matthew 25:31–46. There is no need to be dogmatic. There will be reaping and judgment; of that we can be sure.

CHAPTER 47

THE PRELUDE TO THE BOWLS OF WRATH, A CEREMONY. REVELATION 15

1. Read the entire chapter; it is only eight verses. Where does this scene take place?

   a. In heaven
   b. On earth

2. When does this scene take place?

   a. At the end of the seventieth week, after the trumpets and just before the bowls
   b. In the middle of the seventieth week
   c. At the beginning of the tribulation

We are once again at the end of our timeline. The trumpets have been blown, and the bowls, the last plagues, are about to be poured. This is a very solemn, beautiful ceremony that takes place before the final judgments, the bowls, are poured out on the earth.

3. Why are these the last plagues (15:1)?

   Because "with them the w_____ of God is f_____."

In His grace and mercy, God completes His wrath.

There are actually two scenes depicted in chapter 15; one is of humans, and one is of angels. Both groups are in heaven.

4. Read 15:2–4. These are humans who refused the mark of the beast, standing beside a sea of glass. (Refer back to Revelation 4:6 when we were in the throne room.)

5. What is so special about this group (15:2)?

   They "had c_____ the b_____ and its image and
   the n_____ of its name."

6. It is not stated in the text, but how do you think they conquered it?

   _____

They didn't take the mark of the beast, the number of his name, 666, on their right hand or forehead. We know from Revelation 13:15 that they would have been slain because they wouldn't take it, and yet in their refusal to take the mark, they conquered the beast.

7. Now, since the mark of the beast will be enforced from the middle of the seventieth week on, who comprises this group of brave believers?

   a. Martyrs/overcomers from the church before the resurrection or rapture
   b. Martyrs/overcomers after the rapture, those who become believers during the day of the Lord

Again, it isn't stated here, but both of these groups would have had to take the mark and worship the beast to avoid being slain. They are so precious in God's sight that they are privileged to stand around the sea of glass and sing the song of Moses and of the Lamb.

8. Read Revelation 15:3–4 and sing it to the Lord.

The judgment and wrath yet to be poured on the earth, though horrible, is just and true, for He alone is holy.

9. Read 15:5–8. Sketch the angels and their activity.

Imagine seven beautiful angels emerging from the sanctuary in heaven and one of the four living creatures passing out the bowls of wrath. The glory and power of God and the solemnity of the ceremony prior to the outpouring of the final phase of His wrath leave one breathless.

Answer Key: 1. a
2. a
7. a, b

CHAPTER 48

THE SEVEN BOWLS OF WRATH. REVELATION 16

1. Read chapter 16:1–11. A loud voice from the temple (in heaven) tells the seven angels to "go and p_____ out on earth the seven bowls of the wrath of God" (16:1).

Fill in the chart below regarding the first five bowls.

	1	2	3	4	5
Effects	People who worship image of beast/ marked				
Results	Sores				

After finishing your chart, pause to consider and discuss the state of the earth and its inhabitants after these first five bowls have been poured. People are covered in boils, the oceans are dead, there is no fresh water, the stench on earth is probably horrific, the sun is scorching them, and then they are plunged into darkness. Then it gets worse.

2. Read 16:12–16. What does the sixth bowl effect?

The river E_____.

What happens to the river? _____

In this curious scene, the dragon, beast, and false prophet enlist the help of demons—frog-like spirits who perform signs and gather the kings of the world for a battle they will lose mightily.

They assemble them at a place called A_____.

Armageddon is an actual place; you can find it on your Bible map, and if you go to Israel, you will see it. It is a beautiful, fertile plane, twenty-five by fourteen miles long. It is known as the Jezreel Valley today. It looks like a patchwork quilt with different crops neatly planted at the foot of Mount Megiddo. In Hebrew, the place is known as Har Megiddo—Armageddon. If you stand on the hills of Nazareth, you can gaze over it just as Jesus must have done as a boy, all the while knowing He would fight the final battle there with but a word from His mouth.

We don't see the outcome of this gathering of kings for a battle until 19:17–21. Suffice it to say, it doesn't end well for them.

3. Read 16:17–21. The seventh and final bowl is thrown into the air. Notice that there is no interlude between this bowl and the sixth as there was between the six and seventh seals and trumpets. There is no pause here; things are moving too rapidly. What does the voice from the throne say?

"I_____ i_____ d_____!"

4. What happens when this bowl is poured out (16:18–19)?

Lightning, thunder, and the greatest e_____ in history.

5. While the cities of the nations fall, the great city (presumably Jerusalem, 16:19) is split into how many parts?

_____

This may well be what is described in Zechariah 14.

6. How many mountains and islands are affected?

a. All of them
b. None

7. How many islands are affected?

    a. All of them
    b. None

And if the upheaval of the entire topography of planet earth hasn't affected absolutely everyone, the _____ pound hailstones that fall on them will.

8. What is the reaction of the people?

    They c_____ God.

9. What do you think is the purpose of the increasing intensity of God's wrath, and why is it depicted in bowls?

    _____.

Bowls were used in temple worship and daily life for cleaning and ceremonial cleansing.[40] It seems they are poured out rapidly because God is about to usher in a new day. The earth must be cleansed of the old and the evil.

The time frame for the bowls would, it seems, of necessity be short. The conditions they bring about are simply not compatible with life. As we speculated in our study of Daniel, the bowls may account for those extra thirty days mentioned in the last verses of Daniel.

The bowls full of the wrath of God are horrific, but they are just and true. They are what is deserved. They are what we should receive were it not for the blood of the Lamb.

Answer Key: 6. a
             7. a

---

[40] Howard and Rosenthal, *Feasts of the Lord.* 55

CHAPTER 49

THE GREAT PROSTITUTE AND THE BEAST. REVELATION 17

This is a highly symbolic chapter, but much of the symbolism is explained within the text. Read it carefully and be advised, as verse 9 says, "This calls for a mind with wisdom." It seems that one of the bowl angels wants to show John something—the judgment of Babylon mentioned earlier in 16:19.

1. Read 17:1–6. Sketch and label the scene depicted in verses 3–6.

The prostitute, Babylon, is riding on the Antichrist. The scene you just drew would be humorous if not so disgusting and real as a depiction of a lustful, godless society with false religion having been responsible for the blood of the martyrs of Jesus.

2. Skip ahead and read verses 17:16–18 to see what happens to this revolting woman.

Who hates her and destroys her?

    a. The beast
    b. The ten horns (kings with the beast)
    c. God

Ha! God uses the beast and his apparent ten-nation coalition to destroy Babylon, the mother of earth's abominations. Perhaps the beast uses her as long as false religion suits his purpose; then he devours and burns her. But this is all under God's control.

3. Read 17:7–14. Here we learn more about the beast, the seven heads and the ten horns, and the kings who will hand over their power to the beast.

First, we learn that those whose names are *not* in the book of life will marvel at the beast.

Why do they marvel (17:8)?

Because "it w_____ and is n_____ and is to c_____."

(Recall chapter 13, where we learned that the beast had a mortal wound that was healed—Satan's cheap copy of resurrection.)

Earlier, verse 8 says the beast is *about* to rise from the bottomless pit. The angel may show John the spiritual condition of the world *before* Antichrist becomes apparent.

Second, the seven heads of the beast are said to depict seven mountains or seven kings. John is told that five of the kings and their seats of power (mountains) have fallen. He is told that one is, and the other hadn't come onto the stage of history as yet; but when he did, he would remain only a short while. What empire was in power when John wrote from Patmos?

R_____. There had been five empires prior to Rome, all of which persecuted Israel—Egypt, Assyria, Babylon, Media-Persia, and Greece.

We can only speculate as to the seventh empire, but it wasn't in existence at the time of John's writing and would be brief relative to the others. Many scholars say it was Hitler and Nazi Germany. Truly, perhaps no other "king" or kingdom hated the Jews and Israel more.

seven. What is his (its) destiny (17:11)?

D_____.

We don't know whether the seventh king or kingdom has yet come. We do know that the eighth, Antichrist's kingdom, won't appear until the seventh has come and gone.

Third, we read of ten more kings. These aren't the same kings as the "heads"; those were historical kings. These are the horns, kings in power at the same time as the beast, the eighth and final king, and they give their authority to the beast for a brief time. From this, it is commonly understood that there will be a ten-nation coalition that joins up with the Antichrist in the last days.

Recall the ten toes of iron mixed with clay in the book of Daniel and the terrifying beast in Daniel's dream with ten horns and another "little" horn that came up among them, the eleventh. Daniel saw this ten-nation coalition. They briefly handed their power over to the beast to make war with the Lamb.

5. Read 17:14. Who is with the Lamb, the Lord of lords and King of kings, when He conquers them?

   Those … c_____ and c_____ and f_____.

Oh Lord, we want to be in that number. Thank You for calling and choosing us. Make us faithful.

CHAPTER 50

A BALLAD OF THE FALL OF BABYLON. REVELATION 18

1. Read chapter 18 and then read Isaiah 21:9. From the following words, circle those you would associate with Babylon.

luxury	compassion	simple life	humility
pride	jewels	kindness	joy
excess of food drunkeness	evil	wealthy	sorcery
insatiable	arrogant	contentment	love
lust	deception	peace	patience
immorality	opulence	corruption	kindness
self-control	deception		

Add your own.

181

Way back in Genesis 10–11 in the land of Shinar under Nimrod, king of Babel, mankind decided they would approach God on their own terms. They built a tower to heaven, and God intervened. That tower was known as the Tower of Babel, and Babylon has come to represent everything we want *not* to be because truly anything but the worship of Christ just boils down to the worship of self, empty decadence.

2. How quickly is Babylon destroyed (18:17)?

   In a s_____ h_____.

3. Who mourns over her (18:9, 11, and 17)?

   _____

4. Why do you think those groups mourn?

   _____

5. Who rejoices over her demise (18:20)?

   H_____,   s_____,   a_____
   and p_____.

At the end of history, Babylon still represents the seat of immorality, empty wealth, decadence, and deception. Her destruction will be cause for great rejoicing among God's people.

6. Read 18:4–5. What does the voice from heaven advise?

   Come o_____ of her m_____ people, lest you take part in her s_____ …
   heaped high as h_____.

The ancient desire of people to reach heaven on their own terms culminated in sin, piled as high as the heavens. We want *no* part of "her."

CHAPTER 51

A MARRIAGE SUPPER AND THE RIDER ON A WHITE HORSE. REVELATION 19

1. Read 19:1–5. The chapter opens with the great multitude in heaven rejoicing over the judgment of the prostitute, Babylon. As they cry out "Hallelujah," the twenty-four elders and the four living creatures join them. The beautiful word *hallelujah* is seen only in this particular chapter of the entire New Testament.

2. Read 19:6–9. The marriage of the Lamb has come. Who has made herself ready?

   The b_____.

What is she granted to wear?

   Fine l_____, bright and p_____.

What does the fine linen stand for?

   _____

Even those deeds are granted to her because we have no righteousness apart from the Lamb.

3. Who is the bride?

   The c_____, Us!

(See Ephesians 5:25–27 for Paul's explanation of Christ and His church as the bride.)

In verse 9, the angel tells John to write, "Blessed are those who are i_____ to the marriage supper of the Lamb." At first glance, that statement would seem simple; all those who go to the supper are blessed. However, many scholars speculate that, because brides aren't invited to their own wedding, that this inclusion of others may be the Old Testament saints. The word for *invited* is *kaleo* in Greek, and it means to call, to bid.[41] Everyone present at this wonderful feast will be His called, chosen, and cherished possession.

4. Following this, we see a scene that troubles us. In verse 10, what does John do?

_____(!)

The beloved apostle John falls at the feet of the angel to worship him. Was he just so enthralled with all that was happening that he fell down to worship? We don't know, but we do see this member of the heavenly host scold John and make it plain that only God is to be worshipped.

Now we come to Jesus on His white horse. No humble donkey this time; when rulers came on donkeys, it was for peace. When they came on horses, it was to conquer. And conquer He does.

5. Read 19:11–18. Sketch and label what John sees when heaven opens. It may help to refer back to your drawing of Jesus in chapter 1.

6. Several of His names are mentioned. List them below.

F_____.
T_____.
The W_____ of G_____.
Name only known to H_____.
K_____ of K_____.
L_____ of L_____.

7. The armies of heaven, presumably the bride, because of the fine linen they wear (that was granted to her back in verse 8), are following Him. What are the armies (the believers) riding (19:14)?

W_____ h_____.

Even if you can't ride horses here on earth, you will in heaven.

_____

[41] Zodhiates, *Hebrew-Greek Key*, 1636

8. Read 19:15. Jesus is shown here as the Judge.

   He will rule the nations with "a r_____ of i_____." This is the fulfillment of Psalm 2.

9. Now read 19:17–21 and draw the events in comic-strip style. You are actually depicting the battle of Armageddon.

10. In a macabre contrast to the wedding supper of the Lamb, this horrifying invitation to birds to come and eat the dead (before they have been killed) is shocking but deserved. It demonstrates Christ's sure victory. After the beast and false prophet are thrown alive into the lake of fire, how do the rest die (19:21)?

   a. Those of us on our white horses, the armies of heaven, battle it out with them.
   b. By the sword that comes from the mouth of Jesus
   c. By but a word from Him

Notice that Jesus needs no help.

With the opening of the scroll, the Lord's wrath is on the earth during the trumpets and then the bowls. The bowls change and cleanse the earth. Babylon has been destroyed, and the beast and false prophet are now in the lake of fire. All their followers have been killed, and the birds have feasted. Jesus reigns, and heaven rejoices. The seventieth week is completed. The bowls, perhaps lasting only an extra thirty days, have cleansed the world and now begin a new age.

CHAPTER 52

THE THOUSAND YEARS, THE TORMENT OF SATAN, AND THE GREAT WHITE THRONE. REVELATION 20

1. Read all chapter 20 and order the events in their correct sequence.

   a. The souls of those beheaded come to life and reign with Christ for one thousand years.
   b. An angel comes down from heaven with a chain and the key to the bottomless pit.
   c. Satan is released for a little while.
   d. Satan is bound and thrown in the pit for one thousand years.
   e. The great white throne judgment
   f. Fire comes from heaven to destroy the nations Satan deceived, Gog and Magog.
   g. Satan is thrown into the lake of fire with his buddies, the beast and the false prophet.

You should have b, d, a, c, f, g, e

Many brilliant, reliable, godly scholars don't take the thousand years, commonly called "the millennium," literally. But since our purpose throughout this study has been to learn the content for what it says, we will continue in that vein.

A face-value rendering of this passage places Christ as reigning on earth for one thousand years, while Satan is bound. A golden, peaceful, prosperous age for Israel is repeatedly promised throughout the Old Testament.

We're not told much about the events during that thousand years except that those who were beheaded for Jesus will reign with Him for a thousand years. As to who will enter the millennium, they would have to be believers who trusted Christ during the day of the Lord and miraculously didn't die during it. This would include the one hundred forty-four thousand and those saved due to their witness; those saved among the woman, Israel, who was protected in the wilderness; and possibly some survivor types, who lived and trusted Christ. We can only speculate.

Now we come to a disturbing verse.

2. Read 20:7. After the one thousand years, Satan is released. Why (20:8)?

   To d_____ the nations.

3. He gathers them from all over the world, and their number is huge, like the sand of the sea.

They surround the saints and Jerusalem, but what happens to them (20:9)?

   F_____ came down from heaven.

Again, no battle is too big for our God. And though Hollywood and novelists make much of Gog and Magog, they are defeated in a moment. He still doesn't need our help.

4. Whom does Satan join in the lake of fire?

   The b_____ and the f_____ p_____.

5. How long is their torment?

   F_____ and e_____.

You may wonder, as we do, why Satan is released. Why not throw him into the lake of fire at the beginning of the one thousand years?

Our best understanding is that all who enter the millennial kingdom, the thousand-year reign, are saved. They are still in their mortal bodies, since they were neither raptured nor resurrected and translated. They live long lives in mortal bodies, and they reproduce (Isaiah 65). Those born to them will also need to trust Christ as their Savior, or they will be part of the nations that Satan deceives. By allowing Satan to briefly work after the millennium, the unsaved descendants of the original millennial inhabitants will be dealt with. Then the eternal state will begin.

You may also wonder, where are the believers who were made immortal at the resurrection/rapture during the thousand years?

Again, all this is speculation because it isn't stated definitively, but we believers are immortals at this point with perfect, imperishable bodies. Can we go from heaven to the earthly millennial kingdom for field trips? Will we care to? Jesus is still omnipresent, so He is with us, the immortals in heaven, as well as reigning on earth, if all this is literal. We have no idea, and that is probably divine providence. We know all we need to know, but it *would* make for a good novel. Now we come to the most solemn ceremony in the Bible, the great white throne judgment.

6. Read 20:11–15. What flees from the presence of Him who is seated on the throne?

   E_____ and s_____.

Nothing is left but Him.

7. Who stands before that throne?

   The d_____.

These are the lost dead who have been in hell or Hades until this moment. They are resurrected for this judgment. This is apparently the second resurrection Jesus spoke of in John 5:28–29. "An hour is coming when *all* who are in the tombs will hear his voice and come out, those who have done good to the resurrection of life, and those who have done evil to the resurrection of judgment" (emphasis added).

We also saw this resurrection in Daniel 12:2. "Those who sleep in the dust of the earth shall awake, some to everlasting life and some to shame and everlasting contempt." There are two separate resurrections, separated by a little over one thousand years. The first was at Christ's return when believers were either resurrected or raptured and changed in the twinkling of an eye. A face-value reading of Revelation 20 places this resurrection much later, after the thousand years, as the last event before the eternal state begins (but this timeline issue is highly debatable). This resurrection isn't a second chance for the lost dead, only a reckoning. No saved people are in attendance.

There are books (plural), and there is a book (singular). Both sets are opened.

8. What is written in the books (plural) (20:12–13)?

   What they had d_____.

Much like what happened at the judgment seat of Christ for believers, there will be an accounting. This serves as a review of the lives of the unbelievers.

Many unsaved people have done unspeakably evil deeds, but many are kind and moral, and do good things. These will all be accounted for.

9. But what is the criteria by which they are thrown into the lake of fire (20:15)?

    If their name "was not found written in the b_____ of life."

The book (singular) of life is the Lamb's book of life.

It is often said that works don't work. One's position in Christ is the only criterion for salvation. We cannot write our names in the book of life. That is something the Lamb does for us. Again, works never work. We are saved in Christ alone, by His grace alone, through faith alone—and even that isn't of ourselves; it is a gift from God (Ephesians 2:8–9).

10. Read 20:15. Those whose names weren't found in the book of life were thrown where?

    The lake of f_____.

Does this leave you as speechless as it does us? Knowing this, knowing what our sin deserves, knowing from what we have been saved by His grace, and knowing the ultimate penalty for those who don't know Him—this truth takes our breath away and spurs us on with the privilege of sharing His wonderful good news.

CHAPTER 53

NEW HEAVEN, NEW EARTH, AND THE NEW JERUSALEM. REVELATION 21

1. Read chapter 21 aloud. It's beautiful.

This chapter opens with the word *then*. Just as Revelation 20:11 begins with *then*, placing the great white throne judgment after the millennium, many take this use of *then* to place the new heaven and new earth *after* the millennium and also the great white throne.

First, we will concentrate on the new Jerusalem of verses 1–2 and 9–21. The angel seems eager to show John the bride, the wife of the Lamb, the beautiful city full of God's people. Others have done the math, and according to the dimensions given, the city is fourteen hundred miles high and wide; it's a perfect cube, capable of holding all of us throughout the ages.

Try to draw this "bride," labeling the foundation and gates with the names of the apostles and tribes.

2. What is *not* in this city? Read carefully and list the items below.

We came up with things like tears, death, the sexually immoral, sorcerers, the sun, the moon, night, and a temple.

3. Where or from whom does light come (21:23)?

   The g_____ of G_____.

4. What does He seem to delight in saying?

Write down verses 5–6.

_____

_____

_____

5. And again, what is the requirement for entrance into this holy city (21:27)?

   That my name be "written in the L_____ book of l_____."

Do you *want* your name to be written in that book? He will never turn away anyone who comes by faith, desiring Him. If you're not sure, ask Him right now. Trust Him with your eternity. Surrender. We are all sinners in desperate need of a Savior. He took the wrath as God's Lamb, the perfect Lamb, in our place.

CHAPTER 54

AMEN. COME, LORD JESUS! REVELATION 22

And so we come to the final chapter of the entire Word of God.

1. Read chapter 22. It also is beautiful. Now sketch and label verses 1–5. You are depicting heaven.

2. What is written on our foreheads (22:4)?

   His n_____.

3. What do we *finally* get to see?

   His f_____.

Oh, don't you long to see His face?

4. In 22:6–21, Jesus states many important truths. Record His words in verses 7, 12, and 20.

   _____

   _____

When is Jesus coming?

   S_____ !

Amen. Come, Lord Jesus!

SEQUENCE OF EVENTS AND THEIR IMPACT ON EACH CHARACTER OR GROUP

Fill in the sequence line below, using all you have learned from the New Testament, the Old Testament prophecies, and The Revelation. The seventieth week will have various effects on each character or group at various times. Label each line accordingly, and the layers of information will unfold God's plan for the ages before your eyes.

Tribulation	**Great Tribulation**	**Day of the Lord**

Jesus

_____•_____

Believers/true church

_____•_____

Apostate church/marked

_____•_____

The lost/unsaved/marked

_____•_____

Jews who refuse mark

_____•_____

Jews who take the mark

_____•_____

One hundred forty-four thousand Jewish men

_____•_____

The woman flees to wilderness

_____ • _____

The two witnesses

_____ • _____

Innumerable multitude in heaven

_____ • _____

Martyrs under altar/heaven

_____ • _____

Elijah

_____ • _____

Michael

_____ • _____

Israel

_____ • _____

Satan

_____ • _____

Beast/Antichrist/abomination of desolation/man of lawlessness

_____ • _____

False prophet

_____ • _____

Babylon

_____ • _____

Now label the sequence line below with the events after the seventieth week in whatever way you see the thousand years and the new heavens and new earth.

_____

We have so very much to look forward to. We are looking forward to eternity with you! Sincerely, Dale and Cathy

Dear Heavenly Father,

Our hearts are full of You. Knowing that You are the Alpha and the Omega, that You are forever on Your throne, that You love us with an everlasting love, that You took our place, that You made a way where there was no other way for us to spend a glorious eternity with You, we thank You with all that we have and all that we are. We love You. In the precious, priceless, matchless name of our soon-coming King, Jesus. Amen.

BIBLIOGRAPHY

http://www.biblestudytools.com/commentaries/Revelation/related topics/Jewish wedding analogy. html

ESV Study Bible. Good News Publishers, 2008

https://google.com/templemountfaithful.org/Temple Mount and Land of Israel Faithful Movement, 1997-2020

Google.com/sciencedailey.com/priestly gene shared by widely dispersed jews/July 14, 1998

Howard, Kevin and Marvin Rosenthal, *The Feasts of the Lord*, Orlando, Florida: Zions Hope, Inc. 1997

King James Bible

NIV Study Bible. Zondervan, 1985

Strong, James. *The New Strong's Exhaustive Concordance of the Bible.* Nashville: Thomas Nelson Publishers, 1995.

Wikipedia, s.v, "History of Zionism" last edited April 2020, http:/en.wikipedia.org/History of Zionism

Wikipedia.org/wiki>Sinners_in_the_Hands/Jonathan Edwards/last edited August 16, 2020

Wright, Paul H. *Rose Then and Now: Bible Map Atlas.* Carta, Jerusalem: Bristol Works, Rose Publishing, 2008

Chattanooga, TN: AMG Publishers, 1996

ACKNOWLEDGMENTS

We have worked on this workbook off and on for over twenty years. We listened to the accuser of the brethren *way* too much—telling us we had no business writing it. Finally, in obedience to what we knew God had called us to do and trying not to be concerned that no one would ever read it, we completed it. But not without a great deal of help.

We must first thank Pastor Marvin Rosenthal. Over two decades ago, we discovered his teaching and his Zion's Hope ministry. His soundly biblical, straightforward exegesis of eschatology stirred our hearts and minds, helping to ignite our passion for this study. We were then privileged to take our first trip to Israel with him.

We want to especially thank our dear friend of over three decades, Tracey Buchanan. She was the first person we trusted to see our "baby," and her brilliant and caring editing was vital and indispensable. She took an immature manuscript and made it grow up a bit.

We want to thank Cindy Childs, Christi Perkins, and Anna Shelton. They labored over the manuscript with a fine-tooth comb, editing and reediting—oh, the tedious minutiae of making a workbook look neat and orderly!

And we want thank our pastors and church family, especially the Diggin' In Life Group that we have been privileged to teach for over 25 years. Digging into God's Word together has been a treasured and joyful journey.

The Tribulation, the Great Tribulation, and the Day of the Lord, the Wrath of God

The Seals, Trumpets and Bowls of Revelation

The 70th Week of the Book of Daniel/the covenant of 7 years/Daniel 9

Tribulation-----------(Matt. 24, Mark 13, Luke 21)-----------Great Tribulation-----------(cut short by) **God's Wrath/ Day of the Lord** (2 Peter 3. 1 Thess.4&5)

^Jesus in clouds/dead in Christ resurrected
(1 Thess 4) gathers elect (Matt. 24) rescued

144,000 sealed on earth/Multitude in Heaven

(Rev. 7)

Abomination of Desolation/ holy place (Matt. 24, Daniel 9) J-salem/armies (Luke 21)

Man of Lawlessness in temple of God (2 Thess. 2)

ʌ

*

-----------**Seals** on scroll broken by the Lamb (Rev 6)-----------

#1	#2	#3	#4	#5	#6	#7
Conqueror/	No peace/wars	Famine	¼ earth dies by sword,	Martyrs in Heaven	Cosmic & world	Silence in Heaven (before the)
Antichrist	on earth	$ collapse	famine, plague, beasts	ask "How much longer?"	upheaval	

Trumpets (Rev. 8 &9)

#1 #2 #3 #4 #5 #6 #7

War in Heaven

Michael throws Satan/earth/empowers Beast (AC) 42 mos.

Beast/False Prophet/Mark of the Beast required

Woman/wilderness/3 ½ yrs.

2 witnesses 1,260 days   (Rev. 11,12,13)

Bowls (Rev. 16)

#1#2#3#4#5#6#7

The Tribulation comprises the first 3 ½ years; Great Tribulation & Day of the Lord (duration of either unknown) comprise second 3 ½ years of Daniel's 70th week.

Printed in the United States
By Bookmasters